AQA Science

Exclusively endorsed and approved by AQA

Revision Guide

Pauline Anning • Nigel English • John Scottow

Series Editor: Lawrie Ryan

GCSE Science A

Nelson Thornes
a Wolters Kluwer business

Published in 2006 by:
Nelson Thornes Ltd
Delta Place
27 Bath Road
CHELTENHAM
GL53 7TH
United Kingdom

06 07 08 09 10 / 10 9 8 7 6 5 4 3

A catalogue record for this book is available from the British Library

ISBN 0 7487 8309 1

Cover photographs: snail by Gerry Ellis/Michael Durham/Digital Vision LC (NT), flames by Photodisc 29 (NT), wave by Corel 391 (NT)

Cover bubble illustration by Andy Parker

Illustrations by Bede Illustration, Kevin Jones Associates and Roger Penwill

Page make-up by Wearset Ltd

Printed in Croatia by Zrinski

Acknowledgements

Alamy/Adam Woolfit 64, /**Adrian Sherratt** 46, /**Rob Walls** 62t; **Corbis V98 (NT)** 12; **Corel 11 (NT)** 9b; **Corel 18 (NT)** 34; **Corel 250 (NT)** 65; **Corel 437 (NT)** 47; **Corel 467 (NT)** 38; **Corel 511 (NT)** 9t; **Corel 588 (NT)** 10b; **Corel 640 (NT)** 75tr, 81; **Corel 706 (NT)** 32; **David Buffington/Photodisc 67 (NT)** 7; **Digital Vision 7 (NT)** 37; **Digital Vision 9 (NT)** 95, 107; **Digital Vision 15 (NT)** 23br, 54; **Gerry Ellis/Digital Vision JA (NT)** 24; **Jim Breithaupt** 75mr, 86; **Karl Ammann/Digital Vision AA (NT)** 25t; **Photodisc 29 (NT)** 39; **Photodisc 50 (NT)** 4; **Photodisc 54 (NT)** 18; **Photodisc 67 (NT)** 8, 85; **Science Photo Library** 16, /**Adam Hart-Davis** 26tr, /**Andrew Lambert** 61, /**Andrew McClenaghan** 66, /**Anthony Mercieca** 25m, /**BSIP VEM** 11, /**CNRI** 14b, 14m, /**Cordelia Molloy** 17bl, 59, /**David Nunuk** 27, /**Div. of Computer Research and Technology**, National Institute of Health 23tr, 29, /**Kenneth W. Fink** 35, /**Kent Wood** 17tl, /**Lawrence Lawry** 62mr, /**Martin Bond** 55, /**Martyn F. Chillmaid** 84, /**Maximillian Stock LTD** 82, /**NASA/ESA/STScl** 104, /**Pascal Goetgheluck** 50, /**Renee Lynn** 26b, /**Steve Gschmeissner** 28, /**Tony Craddock** 15; **Stockbyte 29 (NT)** 62bl; **Topfoto.co.uk/National Pictures** 13, /**The Image Works** 10t

Many thanks for the contributions made by Paul Lister, Ann Fullick, Patrick Fullick and Jim Breithaupt.

Picture research by Stuart Sweatmore, Science Photo Library and johnbailey@ntworld.com.

Every effort has been made to trace all the copyright holders, but if any have been overlooked the publisher will be pleased to make the necessary arrangements at the first opportunity.

How to answer questions

Question speak

Command word or phrase	What am I being asked to do?
compare	State the similarities and the differences between two or more things.
complete	Write words or numbers in the gaps provided.
describe	Use words and/or diagrams to say how something looks or how something happens.
describe, as fully as you can	There will be more than one mark for the question so make sure you write the answer in detail.
draw	Make a drawing to show the important features of something.
draw a bar chart / graph	Use given data to draw a bar chart or plot a graph. For a graph, draw a line of best fit.
explain	Apply reasoning to account for the way something is or why something has happened. It is not enough to list reasons without discussing their relevance.
give / name / state	This only needs a short answer without explanation.
list	Write the information asked for in the form of a list.
predict	Say what you think will happen based on your knowledge and using information you may be given.
sketch	A sketch requires less detail than a drawing but should be clear and concise. A sketch graph does not have to be drawn to scale but it should be the appropriate shape and have labelled axes.
suggest	There may be a variety of acceptable answers rather than one single answer. You may need to apply scientific knowledge and/or principles in an unfamiliar context.
use the information	Your answer **must** be based on information given in some form within the question.
what is meant by	You need to give a definition. You may also need to add some relevant comments.

Diagrams

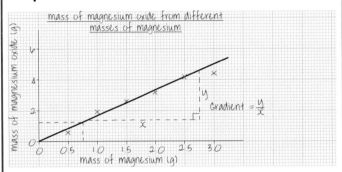

Things to remember:

- Draw diagrams in pencil.
- The diagram needs to be large enough to see any important details.
- Light colouring could be used to improve clarity.
- The diagram should be fully labelled.
- Label lines should be thin and end at the point on the diagram that corresponds to the label.

How long should my answer be?

Things to consider:

1 How many lines have been given for the answer?
   - One line suggests a single word or sentence. Several lines suggest a longer and more detailed answer is needed.

2 How many marks is the answer worth?
   - There is usually one mark for each valid point. So for example, to get all of the marks available for a three mark question you will have to make three different, valid points.

3 As well as lines, is there also a blank space?
   - Does the question require you to draw a diagram as part of your answer?
   - You may have the option to draw a diagram as part of your answer.

Graphs

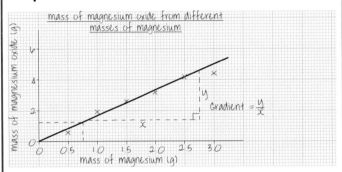

Things to remember:

- Choose sensible scales so the graph takes up most of the grid.
- Don't choose scales that will leave small squares equal to 3 as it is difficult to plot values with sufficient accuracy on such scales.
- Label the axes including units.
- Plot all points accurately by drawing small crosses using a fine pencil.
- Don't try to draw a line through every point. Draw a line of best fit.
- A line of best fit does not have to go through the origin.
- When drawing a line of best fit, don't include any points which obviously don't fit the pattern.
- The graph should have a title stating what it is.
- To find a corresponding value on the y-axis, draw a vertical line from the x-axis to the line on the graph, and a horizontal line across to the y-axis. Find a corresponding value on the x-axis in a similar way.
- The gradient or slope of a line on a graph is the amount it changes on the y-axis divided by the amount it changes on the x-axis. (See the graph above.)

Calculations

- Write down the equation you are going to use, if it is not already given.
- If you need to, rearrange the equation.
- Make sure that the quantities you put into the equation are in the right units. For example you may need to change centimetres to metres or grams to kilograms.
- Show the stages in your working. Even if your answer is wrong you can still gain method marks.
- If you have used a calculator make sure that your answer makes sense. Try doing the calculation in your head with rounded numbers.
- Give a unit with your final answer, if one is not already given.
- Be neat. Write numbers clearly. If the examiner cannot read what you have written your work will not gain credit. It may help to write a few words to explain what you have done.

How to use the 'How Science Works' snake

The snake brings together all of those ideas that you have learned about 'How Science Works'. You can join the snake at different places – an investigation might start an observation, testing might start at trial run.

How do you think you could use the snake on how marble statues wear away with acid rain? Try working through the snake using this example – then try it on other work you've carried out in class.

Remember there really is no end to the snake – when you reach the tail it is time for fresh observations. Science always builds on itself – theories are constantly improving.

OBSERVATION

I wonder why…

HYPOTHESIS

Perhaps it's because…

PREDICTION

I think that if…

I should be honest and tell it as it is. Does the data support or go against my hypothesis?

Is it a linear (straight line) relationship – positive, negative or directly proportional (starting at the origin)? Or is it a curve – complex or predictable?

Which of these should I use?
- Bar chart
- Line graph
- Scatter graph

RELATIONSHIP SHOWN BY DATA

PRESENTING DATA

Am I going further than the data allows me?

Are the links I have found – causal, by association or simply by chance?

CONCLUSION

Have I given a balanced account of the results?

My conclusion would be more reliable and valid if I could find some other research to back up my results.

Just how reliable (trustworthy) was the data? Would it be more reliable if somebody else repeated the investigation? Was the data valid – did it answer the original question?

EVALUATION

USE SECONDARY DATA

There are still many questions that we cannot answer in science

Should the variables I use be continuous (any value possible), discrete (whole number values), ordered (described in sequence) or categoric (described by words)?

I will try to keep all other variables constant, so that it is a fair test. That will help to make it valid.

DESIGN

CONTROL VARIABLE

TRIAL RUN

This will help to decide the:
- Values of the variables
- Number of repeats
- Range and interval for the variables

Can I use my prediction to decide on the variable I am going to change (independent) and the one I am going to measure (dependent)?

Are my instruments sensitive enough?

Will the method give me accuracy (i.e. data near the true value)? Will my method give me enough precision (i.e. data with consistent repeat readings)?

I'll try to keep random errors to a minimum or my results will not be precise. I must be careful!

Are there any systematic errors? Are my results consistently high or low?

PREPARE A TABLE FOR THE RESULTS

CARRY OUT PROCEDURE

Are there any anomalies (data that doesn't follow the pattern)? If so they must be checked to see if they are a possible new observation. If not, the reading must be repeated and discarded if necessary.

I should be careful with this information. This experimenter might have been biased – must check who they worked for; could there be any political reason for them not telling the whole truth? Are they well qualified to make their judgement? Has the experimenter's status influenced the information?

I should be concerned about the ethical, social, economic and environmental issues that might come from this research.

The final decisions should be made by individuals as part of society in general.

Could anyone exploit this scientific knowledge or technological development?

TECHNOLOGICAL DEVELOPMENTS

There are questions that science cannot answer at all – such as 'Should we…?' questions.

B1a | Human biology

Checklist

This spider diagram shows the topics in the unit. You can copy it out and add your notes and questions around it, or cross off each section when you feel confident you know it for your exams.

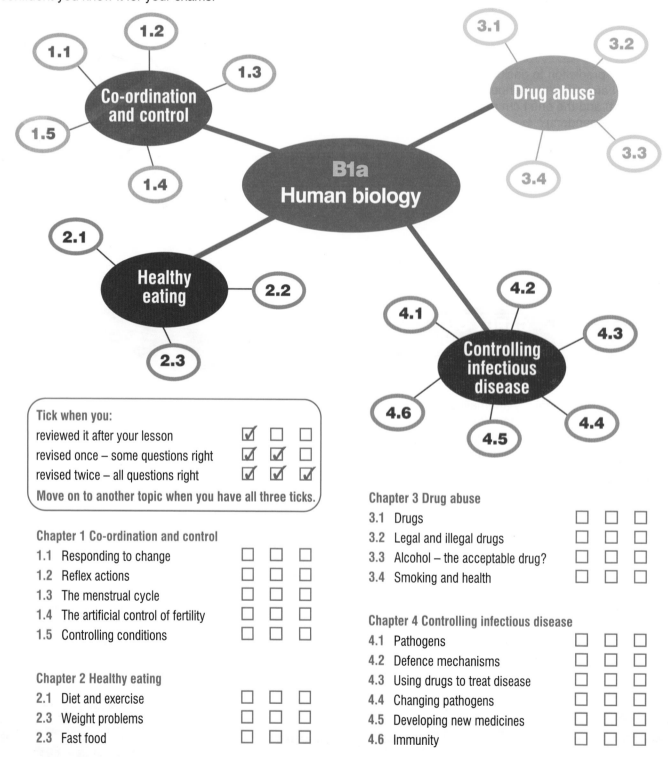

Tick when you:

reviewed it after your lesson	☑	☐	☐
revised once – some questions right	☑	☑	☐
revised twice – all questions right	☑	☑	☑

Move on to another topic when you have all three ticks.

Chapter 1 Co-ordination and control

1.1 Responding to change	☐	☐	☐
1.2 Reflex actions	☐	☐	☐
1.3 The menstrual cycle	☐	☐	☐
1.4 The artificial control of fertility	☐	☐	☐
1.5 Controlling conditions	☐	☐	☐

Chapter 2 Healthy eating

2.1 Diet and exercise	☐	☐	☐
2.3 Weight problems	☐	☐	☐
2.3 Fast food	☐	☐	☐

Chapter 3 Drug abuse

3.1 Drugs	☐	☐	☐
3.2 Legal and illegal drugs	☐	☐	☐
3.3 Alcohol – the acceptable drug?	☐	☐	☐
3.4 Smoking and health	☐	☐	☐

Chapter 4 Controlling infectious disease

4.1 Pathogens	☐	☐	☐
4.2 Defence mechanisms	☐	☐	☐
4.3 Using drugs to treat disease	☐	☐	☐
4.4 Changing pathogens	☐	☐	☐
4.5 Developing new medicines	☐	☐	☐
4.6 Immunity	☐	☐	☐

What are you expected to know?

Chapter 1 Co-ordination and control (See students' book pages 22–35)

- Co-ordination of what happens inside your body, and responses to changes outside your body, rely on hormones and the nervous system.

- The nervous system involves neurones and impulses, which are electrical (except at a synapse).

- A reflex is a rapid, automatic response to a stimulus.

- Internally controlled conditions in your body include:
  - water content
  - ion content
  - temperature
  - blood sugar level.

- Hormones are chemicals produced by glands and carried in your bloodstream.

- The menstrual cycle is controlled by three hormones:
  - follicle stimulating hormone (FSH)
  - oestrogen
  - luteinising hormone (LH).

- These hormones can be used to control a woman's fertility.

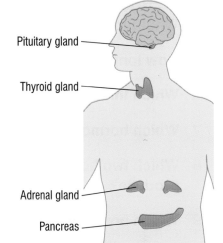

Pituitary gland

Thyroid gland

Adrenal gland

Pancreas

Ovary

Testis

Chapter 2 Healthy eating (See students' book pages 38–45)

- A healthy diet contains the right balance of different foods.

- Too little or too much food can lead to health and weight problems.

- Too much cholesterol or salt can lead to problems in your blood system.

- Cholesterol is carried in the body by low-density lipo-proteins (LDLs are 'bad') or high-density lipo-proteins (HDLs are 'good').

Chapter 3 Drug abuse (See students' book pages 48–59)

- Most drugs harm the body. Even those developed to cure disease can have harmful side effects.

- Drugs can be addictive. If you try to stop taking them you may suffer from withdrawal symptoms.

Chapter 4 Controlling infectious disease (See students' book pages 62–75)

- Microorganisms that cause infection are called 'pathogens'. These include bacteria and viruses.

- The body defends itself by:
  - ingesting pathogens
  - producing antibodies
  - producing antitoxins.

- We can use antibiotics and vaccination to control infection.

- Some pathogens have developed resistance to antibiotics.

1. How are impulses transmitted in the nervous system?

2. Where are hormones produced?

3. What is a synapse?

4. What type of cell detects a change in external conditions, e.g. temperature?

5. How long does the menstrual cycle last?

6. Which three hormones control the cycle?

7. Which hormone stimulates the eggs to be released by an ovary?

8. Which two hormones, controlling the menstrual cycle, does the pituitary gland produce?

9. Which hormone is used in the contraceptive pill?

10. Which hormone is used in the 'fertility' treatment of women?

---

students' book page 24

B1a 1.1   Responding to change

KEY POINT

Control of the body's functions and responses involves hormones (chemicals) and the nervous system (electrical impulses).

The body must respond to internal and external conditions.

- You have glands that produce hormones. The hormones are transported around your body by the blood.
- Electrical impulses pass along the nervous system.
- All responses must be co-ordinated.

Key words: gland, hormone, impulse, nervous system

BUMP UP YOUR GRADE

Remember that impulses are transmitted by chemicals in the hormone system and electrical impulses in the nervous system.

AQA EXAMINER SAYS…

There are often questions about how the nervous and hormone systems are different.

Make sure that you know!

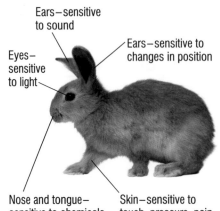

Ears – sensitive to sound

Ears – sensitive to changes in position

Eyes – sensitive to light

Nose and tongue – sensitive to chemicals

Skin – sensitive to touch, pressure, pain and temperature

Being able to detect changes in the environment is important

CHECK YOURSELF

1. How do hormones reach their target organs?

2. What type of organ produces hormones?

3. How are impulses passed along the nervous system?

B1a 1.2 Reflex actions

Here are the steps involved in a reflex action:

- A receptor detects a stimulus (e.g. sharp pain).
- A sensory neurone transmits the impulse.
- A relay neurone passes the impulse on.
- A motor neurone is stimulated.
- The impulse is sent to the effector (muscle or gland).
- Action is taken.

At the junction between two neurones is a synapse. Chemicals transmit the impulse across the gap.

Key words: effector, receptor, neurone, synapse, stimulus

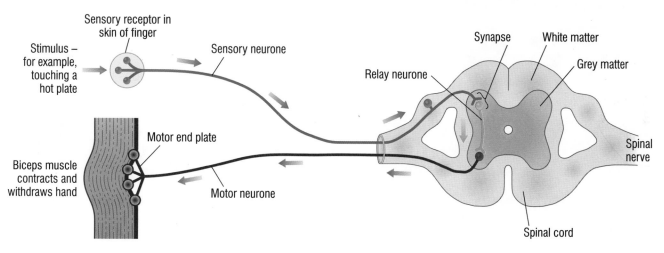

The reflex action which moves your hand away from something hot can save you from a nasty burn!

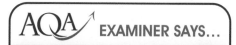
CHECK YOURSELF

1 How are impulses transmitted across a synapse?

2 What is the function (job) of a relay neurone?

3 What are 'effectors'?

B1a 1.3 The menstrual cycle

- **FSH** is made by the pituitary gland and causes the egg to mature and oestrogen to be produced.
- **Oestrogen** is produced by the ovaries and inhibits the further production of FSH. It stimulates the production of LH and also stimulates the womb lining to develop to receive the fertilised egg.
- **LH** is made by the pituitary gland and stimulates the mature egg to be released.

Key words: stimulate, inhibit, womb, mature

AQA EXAMINER SAYS...

Many students remember the effect each hormone has on egg production but forget how each hormone affects the production of the others. Make sure that you know!

GET IT RIGHT!

Remember what each hormone does during the cycle, especially the effect each one has on the production of other hormones.

CHECK YOURSELF

1 Where is FSH produced?
2 What effect does the production of oestrogen have on the production of FSH and LH?
3 What does LH do?

B1a 1.4 The artifical control of fertility

- The contraceptive pill contains oestrogen. This prevents the production of FSH so no eggs mature.
- If a woman cannot produce mature eggs then FSH can be given. This is known as 'fertility treatment'.

Key words: contraception, fertility treatment

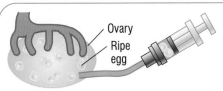

Ovary
Ripe egg

1 Fertility drugs are used to make lots of eggs mature at the same time for collection

2 The eggs are collected and placed in a special solution in a petri dish

3 A sample of semen is collected

4 The eggs and sperm are mixed in the petri dish

5 The eggs are checked to make sure they have been fertilised and the early embryos are developing properly

6 When the fertilised eggs have formed tiny balls of cells, 1 or 2 of the tiny embryos are placed in the uterus of the mother. Then, if all goes well, at least one baby will grow and develop successfully.

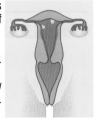

New reproductive technology using hormones and IVF (*in vitro* fertilisation) has helped thousands of infertile couples to have babies

EXAM HINTS

There are issues involved in contraception and fertility treatment. Make sure that you can offer opinions on these issues in an examination. If you only offer a 'one-sided' argument, you may lose up to half of the marks.

CHECK YOURSELF

1 Which hormone is present in the contraceptive pill?
2 Why is FSH used for fertility treatment?

B1a 1.5 Controlling conditions

KEY POINTS

1 It is very important that the internal conditions of the body are kept within certain limits.

2 Water and ion content, as well as temperature and blood sugar level, are all carefully controlled.

A real help in sport – or a good way of making money? Sports drinks are becoming more and more popular, but do most of us really need them?

Internal conditions that are controlled include:

- water content
- ion content
- temperature
- blood sugar level.

Water is leaving the body all the time as we breathe out and sweat. We lose any excess water in the urine (produced by the kidneys). We also lose ions in our sweat and in the urine.

We must keep our temperature constant otherwise the enzymes in the body will not work properly (or may not work at all).

Sugar in the blood is the energy source for cells. The level of sugar in our blood must be controlled.

Key words: internal conditions, blood sugar, ions

CHECK YOURSELF

1 How do we lose water?

2 Why is it important to control our temperature?

3 Why is sugar in the blood important?

B1a 1 End of chapter questions

1 **Describe briefly the stages of a reflex action.**

2 **What are the differences between the hormone and nervous systems?**

3 **What are the functions (jobs) of FSH, oestrogen and LH?**

4 **Suggest one argument for and one argument against the use of fertility treatment.**

5 **State two internal conditions that need to be controlled.**

6 **Which type of neurone transmits the impulse from a motor to a sensory neurone?**

7 **How does the contraceptive pill work?**

8 **Where is LH produced?**

1. What do we mean by a 'balanced diet'?

2. What does malnourished mean?

3. Give three factors that affect how much energy a person needs.

4. What is meant by 'metabolic rate'?

5. What term is used for people who are very fat?

6. State two diseases linked to being overweight.

7. Where is cholesterol made?

8. What are the two types of lipoproteins that carry cholesterol around the body?

9. Which type of fat increases blood cholesterol level?

10. What condition may result from eating too much salt?

---

students' book
page 38

B1a 2.1 — Diet and exercise

KEY POINTS

1 A healthy diet is made up from the 'right' balance of the different foods that you need.
2 You are malnourished if you do not have a balanced diet.
3 If you take in more energy than you need you may become fat, and this may result in health problems.

Food provides the energy that your body needs to carry out its activities.

Everyone needs a source of energy to survive – and your energy source is your food. Whatever food you eat – whether you prefer sushi, dahl, or roast chicken – most people eat a varied diet that includes everything you need to keep your body healthy.

If you exercise you will need more energy.

Exercise increases the metabolic rate. This is the rate at which your body uses energy needed to carry out chemical reactions.

Athletes who spend a lot of time training and playing a sport will have a great deal of muscle tissue on their bodies – up to 40% of their body mass. So they have to eat a lot of food to supply the energy they need.

If it is warm you will need less energy than when it is cold.

The amount of energy you need depends on many things. For example:

- your size
- your sex
- the amount of exercise you do
- outside temperature
- pregnancy.

Key words: energy, metabolic rate, chemical reactions, malnourished

If you live somewhere really cold, you need lots of high-energy fats in your diet. You need the energy to keep warm!

CHECK YOURSELF

1 What do we mean by 'metabolic rate'?

2 State two conditions which would increase the amount of food (energy) that you need.

3 Suggest why exercise increases the metabolic rate.

Weight problems

AQA EXAMINER SAYS...

When asked for a list, many students will remember one or two things. Try to remember three and pick up that extra mark!

If you take in more energy (food) than you need you will become fat.

If you are very fat you are said to be obese.

In spite of some of the media hype, most people are not obese – but the amount of weight people carry certainly varies a great deal!

Obese people are likely to suffer more from:

● arthritis (worn joints)
● diabetes
● high blood pressure
● heart disease.

If you take in less energy (food) than you need you will lose weight.

In developing countries some people have health problems linked to too little food. These include reduced resistance to infection and irregular periods in women.

Key words: obese, arthritis, diabetes, blood pressure, heart disease

Hundreds of thousands of people around the world suffer from the symptoms of malnutrition and starvation. There is simply not enough food for them to eat.

CHECK YOURSELF

1 What word do we use for people who are very fat?
2 What is 'arthritis'?
3 Give three problems, other than arthritis, which obese people may suffer from.

B1a 2.3 Fast food

GET IT RIGHT!

Make sure that you know which lipoprotein is the good one and which the bad one. It is equally important to know which of the three types of fat will increase the cholesterol level in your body.

Fast food can contain too much salt and fat.

Too much salt can lead to increased blood pressure.

Cholesterol is made by the liver and the amount made depends upon diet and inherited (genetic) factors. We need cholesterol, but too much in the blood leads to an increased risk of disease of the heart and blood vessels.

Two types of lipoproteins carry cholesterol around the body:

- low-density lipoproteins (LDLs), which are 'bad' and can cause diseases
- high-density lipoproteins (HDLs), which are 'good' for you.

Saturated fat in your diet increases your cholesterol level.

Mono-unsaturated and polyunsaturated fats help reduce cholesterol levels.

We can use statins to stop the liver producing too much cholesterol.

Key words: cholesterol, lipoprotein, saturated, mono-unsaturated, polyunsaturated, statin

CHECK YOURSELF

1 What problem can too much salt in the diet cause?

2 What do lipoproteins do in the body?

3 Which types of fat can help to reduce blood cholesterol levels?

When you get cholesterol building up in the wrong place – like the arteries leading to your heart – it can be very serious indeed

B1a 2 End of chapter questions

1 What can a doctor give you to lower your blood cholesterol level?

2 Which type of fat is likely to increase your blood cholesterol level?

3 If you are fat name three conditions you are more likely to suffer from.

4 What is meant by your 'metabolic rate'?

5 Suggest why you might need more energy on a cold day.

6 In developing countries state one health problem people without enough food might suffer from.

7 What is LDL an abbreviation for?

8 What is 'fast food' likely to contain too much of in terms of a person's diet?

1. What does the word 'illegal' mean?

2. Why are new drugs, developed by scientists, always thoroughly tested before the public can use them?

3. Why was thalidomide used?

4. What are 'withdrawal' symptoms?

5. What do we mean by 'recreational' drugs?

6. Name two illegal drugs.

7. Name two very addictive drugs.

8. What is the addictive substance in tobacco smoke?

9. What effect does carbon monoxide have on the body?

10. What effect does alcohol have on the nervous system?

---

students' book page 48   ## B1a 3.1   Drugs

KEY POINTS

1 All drugs can cause problems whether they are illegal or legal.
2 Many drugs are addictive. If you try to stop taking them this can result in severe withdrawal symptoms.

GET IT RIGHT!

Many problems today are caused by legal drugs, e.g. tobacco and alcohol because they are so widely used (and abused).

Useful drugs, made from natural substances, have been used by indigenous people for a very long time.

When we develop new drugs to help people, we have to test them over a long time to make sure that there are no serious side effects.

- Thalidomide was used as a sleeping pill and to prevent morning sickness in pregnant women. It had very serious side effects on fetuses developing in the womb. It is now used to help cure leprosy.

Millions of pounds worth of illegal drugs are brought into the UK every year. It is a constant battle for the police to find and destroy drugs like these.

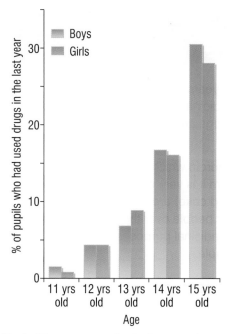

% of pupils who had used drugs in the last year

Boys
Girls

11 yrs old | 12 yrs old | 13 yrs old | 14 yrs old | 15 yrs old

Age

Most of the young people who have used drugs have smoked cannabis – but the number of 15-year-old students who have tried drugs is causing a lot of concern

- Recreational drugs are used by people for pleasure.

- Heroin and cocaine are recreational drugs. They are very addictive and illegal.

- Cannabis is a recreational drug. It is also illegal. It is argued that using cannabis can lead to using 'harder' drugs.

- If you try to stop taking addictive drugs you will suffer withdrawal symptoms.

Key words: illegal, addictive, withdrawal, recreational, indigenous

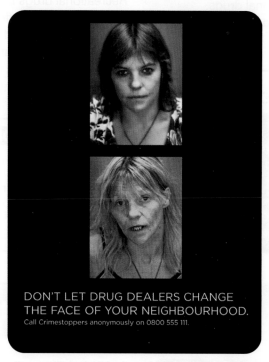

DON'T LET DRUG DEALERS CHANGE THE FACE OF YOUR NEIGHBOURHOOD.
Call Crimestoppers anonymously on 0800 555 111.

Drugs can seem appealing, exciting and fun when you first take them. Many people use them for a while and then leave them behind. But the risks of addiction are high, and no-one can predict who drugs will affect most.

BUMP UP YOUR GRADE

You may get a question in an examination asking whether taking cannabis leads to taking harder drugs. You must try to make both sides of the argument, as there is no 'right' answer. If you *only* make an argument for or against, you will lose up to half of the marks.

CHECK YOURSELF

1 At the present time, what is thalidomide used to help cure?

2 Name one recreational drug.

3 Suggest why legal recreational drugs are possibly more of a problem than illegal ones.

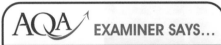

students' book
page 50

B1a 3.2 Legal and illegal drugs

KEY POINTS

1 There are both legal drugs and illegal drugs.
2 There are both medicinal drugs and recreational drugs.
3 Some legal drugs can be used illegally.

AQA EXAMINER SAYS...

Make sure that you know the difference between a drug used as a medicine and a drug that is simply used for pleasure (recreationally). You must also know the difference between legal drugs and illegal drugs.

Medicinal drugs are developed over many years and are used to control disease or help people that are suffering. Many medicinal drugs are only available on prescription from a doctor. Recreational drugs are used only for pleasure and affect the brain and the nervous system.

Recreational drugs include cannabis and heroin which are both illegal. As recreational drugs affect the nervous system it is very easy to become addicted to them. Nicotine and caffeine (in coffee and coke) are legal drugs which are used recreationally, alcohol is also legal for people over the age of 18 in this country. Some drugs which are used for medicinal purposes can be used illegally, e,g, stimulants used by sports people.

CHECK YOURSELF

1 Name one drug used recreationally which is legal.

2 Why can taking recreational drugs lead to addiction?

3 Why do some people say that there is a bigger problem with legal, recreational drugs as opposed to illegal, recreational drugs?

---

students' book
page 52

B1a 3.3 Alcohol – the acceptable drug?

KEY POINTS

1 Alcohol is a legal drug that can be bought by those over 18 years old in the UK.
2 Alcohol does cause serious health problems for some that use it.
3 Alcohol is a 'recreational' drug.

AQA EXAMINER SAYS...

Remember that alcohol is legal. However, it still causes many more problems in our society than illegal drugs such as heroine and cocaine as it is much more widely used.

- Alcohol slows down the nervous system and therefore slows down your reactions. This will cause problems when driving.
- Too much alcohol leads to loss of self control.
- Drinking too much alcohol may cause a person to lose consciousness or go into a coma.
- The use of alcohol over a long time will damage the liver (cirrhosis) and brain.

Key words: alcohol, coma, liver damage, brain damage

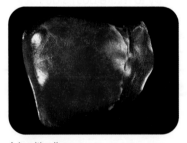

A healthy liver

Your liver deals with all the poisons you put into your body. But if you drink too much alcohol, your liver may not be able to cope. The difference between the healthy liver and the liver with cirrhosis shows just why people are warned against heavy drinking!

CHECK YOURSELF

1 What effect does alcohol have on the nervous system?

2 Which two organs of the body does alcohol damage?

3 Why should you not 'drink and drive'?

Diseased liver from a drinker with cirrhosis

Smoking and health

KEY POINTS

1 Smoking tobacco is legal.
2 The use of tobacco causes a range of health problems and will probably lead to an early death.

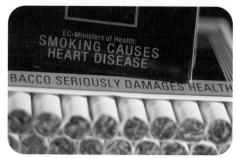

Cigarette smoking increases your risk of developing many serious and fatal diseases. Every packet of cigarettes sold in the UK has to carry a clear health warning. Yet people still buy them in their millions!

- It is not illegal to smoke tobacco over the age of 16 years.
- The nicotine in tobacco smoke is addictive.
- Tobacco smoke also contains cancer causing chemicals (carcinogens).
- The carbon monoxide in tobacco smoke reduces the amount of oxygen the blood can carry.
- Pregnant women who smoke have babies with lower birth weights, as the babies do not get enough oxygen.

Key words: nicotine, tobacco, carcinogen, carbon monoxide

 EXAMINER SAYS...

Remember it is the nicotine in tobacco smoke that is addictive, and other chemicals in the smoke that cause cancer.

GET IT RIGHT!

Babies born to mothers that smoke have low birth weights. The babies receive less oxygen to release the energy from food (in respiration) that they need to grow properly.

CHECK YOURSELF

1 Why can smoking tobacco cause cancer?

2 What is the addictive substance in cigarettes?

3 Why do the babies born to mothers that smoke have lower birth weights?

B1a 3   End of chapter questions

1 What effect does alcohol have on the nervous system?

2 How does carbon monoxide affect the body?

3 Why is it dangerous if you 'drink and drive'?

4 Where do the chemicals that cause lung cancer come from?

5 Why does it take so long for a new medicinal drug to be made available?

6 Give one reason why some people say that taking cannabis can lead to taking 'hard' drugs.

7 What is the general name for a substance that may cause cancer?

8 Name one legal, recreational drug.

1. What is a 'pathogen'?

2. Name two organisms that can act as pathogens.

3. What is the other name for the poisons that pathogens produce?

4. What type of cell produces antibodies?

5. What is an anti-toxin?

6. What do painkillers do?

7. What is an antibiotic?

8. Why is it so difficult to kill viruses?

9. Why is MRSA so dangerous?

10. What is in a vaccine?

---

students' book page 62

B1a 4.1 — Pathogens

KEY POINT

Pathogens are microorganisms that cause infectious disease.

EXAM HINTS

Remember in an exam answer that pathogens reproduce before they make enough toxins to make you feel ill.

BUMP UP YOUR GRADE

You will 'bump' your grade in an exam answer from C/D to A by not just knowing *what* Semmelweiss discovered about the transfer of infection, but *why* it took so long for his ideas to be accepted.

- Pathogens cause infectious disease.
- Some bacteria and viruses are pathogens. These bacteria and viruses reproduce inside the body producing poisons (toxins) that make us feel ill.
- Semmelweiss discovered that infection could be transferred between patients in a hospital. He said that washing your hands between treating patients helped stop the transfer of infection. However, it was many years before other doctors took his ideas seriously.

Key words: pathogen, bacteria, virus, toxin, infectious

Ignaz Semmelweiss – his battle to persuade medical staff to wash their hands to prevent infections is still going on today!

CHECK YOURSELF

1 Name the two microorganisms that can cause infection.

2 How did Semmelweiss suggest that you could control the spread of infection in a hospital?

3 Why did it take so long for others to accept Semmelweiss's ideas?

B1a 4.2 Defence mechanisms

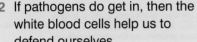

KEY POINTS

1 It is best to stop pathogens getting into your body in the first place, e.g. having no cuts on the skin or trapping pathogens in the mucus in your nose.

2 If pathogens do get in, then the white blood cells help us to defend ourselves.

White blood cells do three things to help us protect ourselves:

● They can ingest pathogens. This means that they digest and destroy them.
● They produce antibodies to help destroy particular pathogens.
● They produce antitoxins to counteract (neutralise) the toxins that pathogens produce.

Key words: white blood cell, ingest, antibody, antitoxin

Droplets carrying millions of pathogens fly out of your mouth and nose at up to 100 miles an hour when you sneeze!

AQA EXAMINER SAYS...

In the exam most students will only remember one or, at most, two things that white blood cells do. Try to remember all three!

GET IT RIGHT!

Never write in an exam that the white blood cells eat the pathogens! They ingest them.

CHECK YOURSELF

1 What is the best way to prevent infection?

2 What do antibodies do?

3 How do antitoxins get rid of toxins?

B1a 4.3 Using drugs to treat disease

KEY POINTS

1 Antibiotics can be used to kill bacteria.
2 It is much more difficult to kill viruses.

● Antibiotics kill infective bacteria in the body. Penicillin is a well-known antibiotic.
● Viruses are much more difficult to kill, as they live inside the cells.
● Painkillers make you feel better, but do nothing to get rid of the disease causing the pain.

Key words: antibiotic, penicillin, painkiller

GET IT RIGHT!

Viruses are harder to get rid of, as they reproduce inside cells. If you destroy the virus you can easily destroy the cell as well.

AQA EXAMINER SAYS...

Remember that painkillers only relieve the symptoms of a disease.

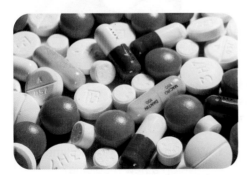

Penicillin was the first antibiotic. Now we have many different types that kill different types of bacteria. In spite of this, scientists are always on the look out for new antibiotics to keep us ahead in the battle against the pathogens.

CHECK YOURSELF

1 What do antibiotics do?

2 Why is it so difficult to get rid of viruses?

3 What is the job of painkillers?

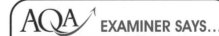

B1a 4.4 Changing pathogens

KEY POINT

If a pathogen changes by mutating or through natural selection, then it will be very difficult to control.

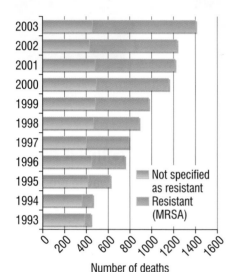

Number of deaths

Legend:
- Not specified as resistant
- Resistant (MRSA)

Source: National Statistics Office

The growing impact of MRSA in our hospitals can be seen from this data

The MRSA 'super bug' is a bacterium that has evolved in hospitals through natural selection. It is resistant to commonly used antibiotics.

Some pathogens, particularly viruses, can mutate resulting in new forms.

Very few people are immune to these new pathogens and so disease can spread quickly within a country (epidemic) or across countries (pandemic).

Key words: natural selection, mutation, epidemic, pandemic

AQA EXAMINER SAYS...

Remember that bacteria don't 'want' to develop resistance – they just do!

Make sure you understand how bacteria become resistant to antibiotics through natural selection.

GET IT RIGHT!

Mutation takes place in an instant, whereas natural selection is a gradual process over many years.

CHECK YOURSELF

1 What is a 'pandemic'?

2 Why is MRSA called a 'super bug'?

3 What is meant by 'natural selection'?

B1a 4.5 Developing new medicines

KEY POINTS

1 A new medicine must be effective, it must be safe and it must be able to be stored for a period of time.
2 New medicines are tested in laboratories to see if they are toxic and on human volunteers to see if they work.

AQA EXAMINER SAYS...

It is important to test new medicines on animals first to see if they are toxic. Some people are against the use of animals for this. In an examination be prepared to argue the case for and against the use of animals in testing new medicines.

It costs a lot of money to develop a new medicine. It also takes a long time. New medicines must be tested to see if they are toxic (poisonous) and to see if they are effective (cure the disease). This work is carried out in laboratories (on animals) and on human volunteers.

If these tests are not thorough enough then a new medicine may have dangerous side effects. Thalidomide is a medicine that was used widely in the 1950s as a sleeping pill. It also helped to prevent 'morning sickness' in pregnant women. It was not tested thoroughly enough and women started to give birth to babies with severe limb abnormalities. It is now not used with pregnant women but is proving an effective treatment for leprosy.

Key words: toxic, side effects, thalidomide

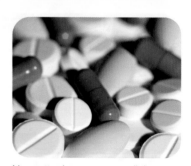

No matter how many medicines we have, there is always room for more as we tackle new diseases!

CHECK YOURSELF

1 Why does it take a long time to develop a new medicine?

2 Why was thalidomide used in the 1950s?

3 Why are some people against the testing of drugs on animals?

Immunity

- Dead or inactive forms of an organism can be made into a vaccine. Vaccines can be injected into the body.
- The white blood cells react by producing antibodies. This makes the person immune and prevents further infection, as the body responds quickly by producing more antibodies.
- There is argument over whether some vaccines are completely safe, e.g. the MMR (measles, mumps and rubella) vaccine.

Key words: vaccine, immune

This is how vaccines protect you against dangerous infectious diseases

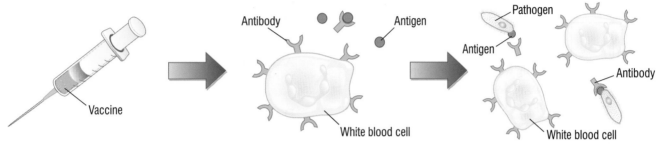

Small amounts of dead or inactive pathogen are put into your body, often by injection.

The antigens in the vaccine stimulate your white blood cells into making antibodies. The antibodies destroy the antigens without any risk of you getting the disease.

You are immune to future infections by the pathogen. That's because your body can respond rapidly and make the correct antibody as if you had already had the disease.

GET IT RIGHT!

A vaccine is made from dead or inactive forms of the pathogen.

CHECK YOURSELF

1 What is meant by 'vaccination'?

2 How does the person vaccinated develop immunity?

3 Why are the forms of the pathogen used dead or inactive?

B1a 4   End of chapter questions

1 **What did Semmelweiss find out?**

2 **Why do pathogens make you feel ill?**

3 **What is a vaccine?**

4 **What is an antibody?**

5 **What is meant when we say that white blood cells 'ingest' pathogens?**

6 **Name a commonly used antibiotic.**

7 **Where in the body do viruses live and reproduce?**

8 **What is meant by the word 'mutation'?**

1 Drugs are widespread in modern-day society. Some are used for our benefit (medicines), but others are used for recreation.

Match words A, B, C and D with statements (i)–(iv) in the table.

A   alcohol
B   cannabis
C   thalidomide
D   heroin

Statement	Description
(i)	this is an illegal recreational, hard drug
(ii)	this is a legal recreational drug
(iii)	this drug was used as a sleeping pill
(iv)	it is argued whether this illegal drug can lead to taking harder drugs

2 The drawing shows a lion.

The lion has organs that contain different receptors.

Match statements A, B, C and D with labels (i)–(iv) on the drawing.

A   contains receptors sensitive to chemicals
B   contains temperature receptors
C   contains light receptors
D   contains sound receptors

3 The diagram gives some information about a woman's monthly cycle.

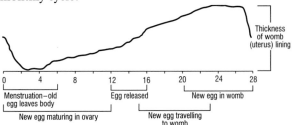

Match numbers labelled A, B, C, and D with statements (i)–(iv) in the table.

A   21
B   13
C   24
D   18

Statement	Description
(i)	a day when the egg is released
(ii)	a day when the womb lining is thickest
(iii)	a day when the new egg could be moving towards the womb
(iv)	a day when the new egg could be in the womb

4 This table shows the effects that substances can have on the body.

Match the words A, B, C and D, with the statements (i)–(iv) in the table.

A   alcohol
B   tobacco
C   cocaine
D   carbon monoxide

Statement	Effect on the body
(i)	may cause damage to the liver
(ii)	may cause lung cancer
(iii)	combines with red blood cells
(iv)	is very addictive

5 The body defends itself against infection. The table shows some ways it can defend itself.

Match words A, B, C and D with the statements (i)–(iv) in the table.

A   blood clot
B   mucus
C   antitoxins
D   antibodies

Statement	What it does
(i)	lines the air passages to trap pathogens
(ii)	neutralises the poisons produced by pathogens
(iii)	seals the skin when it is cut
(iv)	ingests pathogens

6 A–D affect the body, match them with the effects (i)–(iv) in the table.

A   too much salt in the diet
B   too little food to eat
C   a high proportion of saturated fat
D   a high proportion of low density lipoproteins

Test & Assessment Interactive quizzes, answers and hints online!

Number	Effect on the body
(i)	reduces blood cholesterol
(ii)	causes high blood pressure
(iii)	causes heart disease
(iv)	causes irregular periods

7 A person puts their finger down on a pin. They automatically move their hand away. The diagram shows what happens in this reflex arc.

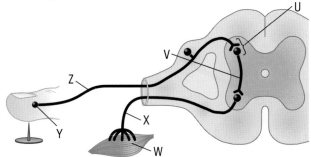

(i) In this reflex action the receptor is found at . . .
  A U
  B V
  C W
  D Y

(ii) In this reflex action a synapse is found at . . .
  A U
  B V
  C W
  D Z

(iii) In this reflex action the motor neurone is found at . . .
  A V
  B X
  C Y
  D Z

(iv) The label V is pointing to . . .
  A a synapse
  B a relay neurone
  C a sensory neurone
  D a muscle

8 Measles can be a very serious disease, caused by a virus.

The MMR vaccine is used to protect children from catching measles, mumps and rubella.

(i) The vaccine contains . . .
  A dead or weakened bacteria
  B antibodies
  C antitoxins
  D dead or weakened viruses

(ii) Some diseases can be treated successfully with antibiotics. Measles cannot be, as. . .
  A the toxins the pathogen produces are too strong
  B the measles virus keeps mutating
  C the virus is inside the body cells
  D the antibodies in the antibiotic are not strong enough

(iii) Vaccines work in the body by . . .
  A trapping the pathogens
  B stimulating white blood cells to produce antitoxins
  C stimulating the white cells to produce antibodies
  D digesting the bacteria

(iv) Vaccines have to be tested over a very long period before they can be used. This is . . .
  A to see whether they are effective against other pathogens
  B to find out how much they really cost
  C to see if there are cheaper alternatives
  D to find out if there are any side effects

9 The menstrual cycle of a woman is controlled by three hormones.

(i) Which organ of the body produces oestrogen?
  A ovary
  B pancreas
  C pituitary
  D liver

(ii) Which of these statements is true of FSH?
  A It is produced by the ovary and causes the uterus to develop.
  B It is produced by the pituitary and inhibits oestrogen production.
  C It is produced by the ovary and inhibits oestrogen production.
  D It is produced by the pituitary and stimulates oestrogen production.

(iii) Which hormone(s) stimulate the release of the mature egg?
  A LH and FSH
  B LH
  C oestrogen and LH
  D FSH

(iv) Oestrogen is used in the contraceptive pill as it . . .
  A stimulates FSH production
  B stimulates LH production and inhibits FSH production
  C inhibits FSH production
  D stimulates the production of both FSH and LH

B1b | Evolution and environment

Checklist

This spider diagram shows the topics in the unit. You can copy it out and add your notes and questions around it, or cross off each section when you feel confident you know it for your exams.

Adaptation for survival — 5.1, 5.2, 5.3, 5.4

Variation — 6.1, 6.2, 6.3, 6.4, 6.5

B1b Evolution and environment

How people affect the planet — 8.1, 8.2, 8.3, 8.4, 8.5

Evolution — 7.1, 7.2, 7.3, 7.4

Tick when you:

reviewed it after your lesson	☑	☐	☐
revised once – some questions right	☑	☑	☐
revised twice – all questions right	☑	☑	☑

Move on to another topic when you have all three ticks.

Chapter 5 Adaptation for survival
5.1 Adaptation in animals ☐ ☐ ☐
5.2 Adaptation in plants ☐ ☐ ☐
5.3 Competition in animals ☐ ☐ ☐
5.4 Competition in plants ☐ ☐ ☐

Chapter 6 Variation
6.1 Inheritance ☐ ☐ ☐
6.2 Types of reproduction ☐ ☐ ☐
6.3 Cloning ☐ ☐ ☐
6.4 New ways of cloning animals ☐ ☐ ☐
6.5 Genetic engineering ☐ ☐ ☐

Chapter 7 Evolution
7.1 The origins of life on Earth ☐ ☐ ☐
7.2 Theories of evolution ☐ ☐ ☐
7.3 Natural selection ☐ ☐ ☐
7.4 Extinction ☐ ☐ ☐

Chapter 8 How people affect the planet
8.1 The effects of the population explosion ☐ ☐ ☐
8.2 Acid rain ☐ ☐ ☐
8.3 Global warming ☐ ☐ ☐
8.4 Sustainable development ☐ ☐ ☐
8.5 Planning for the future ☐ ☐ ☐

What are you expected to know?

Chapter 5 Adaptation for survival (See students' book pages 82–91)

- Organisms (animals and plants) all compete for available resources, e.g. food.

- Animals also compete with each other for mates.

- Animals and plants have adaptations so that they can successfully survive in the areas they live in.

Chapter 6 Variation (See students' book pages 94–105)

- Genetic information from parents is passed on to their offspring.

- This information is carried in the genes present in the sex cells (gametes).

- Different genes control different characteristics.

- There are two types of reproduction – sexual and asexual.

- Various techniques can be used to produce new, identical plants. These include tissue culture and taking cuttings. This is known as 'cloning' and is a type of asexual reproduction.

- Cloning is more difficult with animals, but techniques have been developed including embryo transplants, fusion and adult cell cloning.

- Genetic engineering is now widely used to produce organisms with characteristics that we want.

- There is a lot of argument over the issues of cloning in animals and the genetic engineering of animals and plants.

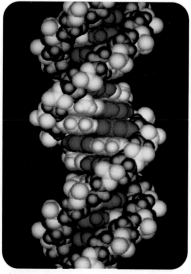

DNA

Chapter 7 Evolution (See students' book pages 108–117)

- Darwin's theory of evolution is now widely accepted (though not by everyone).

- Darwin's theory is based upon variation between members of the same species and the process of natural selection.

- The evidence supporting Darwin's theory includes the fossil record.

- Organisms do become extinct and there are a number of reasons why this happens.

Chapter 8 How people affect the planet (See students' book pages 120–131)

- The human population is growing.

- We are producing much more waste and pollution, and we are also using up the Earth's valuable resources.

- Global warming and the formation of acid rain are two important effects that we are having on the planet.

- There is a lot of effort now being put into 'sustainable development'.

Air pollution

1. State three things that plants compete for.

2. State one other thing that animals compete for.

3. In the Arctic, why might a predator have a white coat in the winter?

4. In the Arctic, why might the prey of a predator have a brown coat in the summer?

5. When answering questions about animals, what do we mean by the 'surface area to volume ratio'?

6. What conditions, in a desert, are likely to cause problems for animals or plants?

7. Why might animals or plants have bright colours?

8. Why do some animals need a territory?

9. In woodland, what might plants be competing for?

10. Why do some plants spread their seed as far away from themselves as possible?

---

students' book page 82

B1b 5.1   Adaptation in animals

KEY POINT

If animals were not adapted to survive in the areas they live in, they would die.

- Animals in cold climates (e.g. in the Arctic) have thick fur and fat under the skin (blubber) to conserve heat.

The Arctic is a cold and bleak environment. However, the animals that live there are well adapted for survival. Notice the large size, small ears, thick coat and white camouflage of this polar bear.

- Some animals in the Arctic (e.g. Arctic fox, Arctic hare) are white in the winter and brown in the summer. This means that they are camouflaged so they are not easily seen.

Many students do not understand surface area to volume ratio. It is a very important idea in science. The larger the animal, the smaller its surface area is compared to its volume.

EXAM HINTS

Adaptations are not just to do with what the animal looks like; some adaptations are about the animal's behaviour.

- Bigger animals have smaller surface areas compared to their volume, this means that they can conserve heat more easily but it is also more difficult to lose heat.

Elephants are pretty big but they live in hot, dry climates. Its huge wrinkled skin would cover an animal which was much bigger still. The wrinkles increase the surface area to aid heat loss.

- In dry conditions (desert) animals are adapted to conserve water and to stop them getting too hot. Animals in the desert may hunt or feed at night so that they remain cool during the day.

Animals like this fennec fox have many adaptations to help them cope with the hot dry conditions. How many can you spot?

Key words: adaptation, conserve, surface area : volume ratio, camouflage

CHECK YOURSELF

1 An elephant has a small surface area compared to its volume. How will this affect it in hot climates?

2 Why do very small animals find it difficult to live in the Arctic?

3 Why are Arctic foxes white in the winter?

Adaptation in plants

KEY POINTS

1 Plants must be adapted to live in a variety of climates, including deserts.
2 Plants must also be adapted to survive being eaten by animals.

EXAM HINTS

There are many ways plants conserve water in dry environments. These include extensive roots, waxy leaves, small leaves and water storage in stems. Don't limit yourself to one idea in an exam!

- Plants compete for light, water and nutrients.
- In dry conditions, e.g. deserts, plants have become very well adapted to conserve water, e.g. cacti.
- Plants are eaten by animals. Some plants have developed thorns, poisonous chemicals and warning colours to put animals off.

Key words: conserve, warning

CHECK YOURSELF

1 Where might small plants find it difficult to receive enough light?

2 State three possible ways a plant might conserve water.

3 How do animals know not to eat certain plants?

Cacti are well adapted to survive in desert conditions

Competition in animals

KEY POINTS

1 Animals compete with each other in many different ways.
2 The most successful ones survive and pass on their genes to the next generation.

AQA EXAMINER SAYS...

There are many ways animals are adapted. Colour (to attract females or as camouflage) and speed to catch food or escape from predators are only two of them.

- Animals compete with each other for water, food, space, mates and breeding sites.
- An animal's territory will be large enough to find water, food and have space for breeding.
- Predators compete with their prey, as they want to eat them.
- Predators and prey may be camouflaged, so that they are less easy to see.
- Prey animals compete with each other to escape from the predators and to find food for themselves.
- Some animals, e.g. caterpillars, may be poisonous and have warning colours so that they are not eaten.

Key words: predator, prey, camouflage

CHECK YOURSELF

1 Why do animals need a territory?

2 Why do warning colours prevent some animals being eaten?

3 How are giraffes adapted to survive?

Cheetahs are highly adapted for speed

Competition in plants

KEY POINTS

1 Plants compete for a number of resources.
2 Successful plants have structures and habits that allow healthy growth.

- All plants compete for water, nutrients and light.
  For example, in woodland some smaller plants (e.g. snowdrops) flower before the trees are in leaf, so that they have enough light, water and nutrients.

- Some plants spread their seeds over a wide area so that they do not compete with themselves.

Key words: nutrients, habits

Coconuts will float for weeks, or even months, on ocean currents which can carry them hundreds of miles from their parents – and any other coconuts!

AQA EXAMINER SAYS...

Plants do have structures to enable them to compete, e.g. extensive root systems. However, in an exam question, it is also important to mention that they may have successful growing habits, e.g. they grow quickly so that they gain as much light as possible, or they grow at a time when other plants are dormant, e.g. snowdrops in a wood.

CHECK YOURSELF

1 What three resources do plants compete for?

2 Why do some plants grow and flower early in a wood?

3 Why would plants want to scatter their seeds away from themselves?

B1b 5 — End of chapter questions

1 How will an animal learn not to eat certain plants?

2 What will members of the same animal species, e.g. tigers, compete for?

3 Why might it be necessary for some predators to be camouflaged?

4 What conditions in a desert are likely to be difficult for plants and animals?

5 Why do whales have a thick layer of blubber under the skin?

6 State one way in which a cactus is adapted to conserve water.

7 Suggest two reasons why some animals in the desert bury themselves in the sand during the day.

8 Suggest one advantage of a pride of lions causing a herd of animals to run before deciding which one to attack.

1. What are gametes?

2. Where in a cell are chromosomes found?

3. What are chromosomes made up from?

4. Why does sexual reproduction lead to variation in the offspring?

5. How is asexual reproduction different to sexual reproduction?

6. Why are cuttings taken from a plant the same as the parent plant?

7. How do you grow new plants using tissue culture?

8. What does 'cloning' mean?

9. In genetic engineering, how are genes 'cut out' of the chromosome?

10. Why are there arguments about whether genetic engineering should be allowed?

---

students' book page 94 | ## B1b 6.1 | Inheritance

● The cell nucleus contains chromosomes.

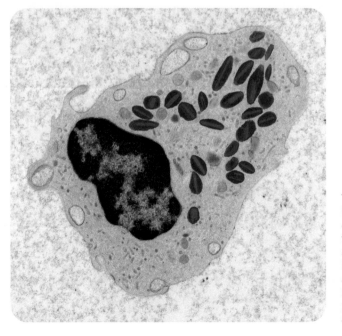

This micrograph shows a highly magnified human cell. In fact the nucleus of the cell would only measure about 0.005 mm! All the instructions for making you and keeping you going are inside this microscopic package. It seems amazing that they work!

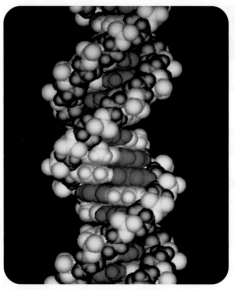

DNA! This huge molecule is actually made up of lots of smaller molecules joined together. Each gene is a small section of the big DNA strand.

- Chromosomes are made up of genes.
- The male and female sex cells (gametes) contain the genes so the genetic information is passed on to the offspring.
- Genes control the development of the characteristics of the offspring.

Key words: nucleus, chromosome, gene, gamete

GET IT RIGHT!

It is the individual genes that control the characteristics of the offspring. Chromosomes are simply *made up* of genes.

CHECK YOURSELF

1 What do genes control?

2 How is genetic information passed from parents to offspring?

3 In which part of a cell are chromosomes found?

B1b 6.2 Types of reproduction

KEY POINTS

1 There are two types of reproduction – sexual and asexual.

2 There are very important differences between sexual and asexual reproduction.

AQA EXAMINER SAYS...

Many students forget why one type of reproduction results in variation and the other doesn't. It is simply that in sexual reproduction genes are mixed from the two parents, whereas in asexual reproduction there is only one parent so mixing is impossible!

- Sexual reproduction involves the fusion of sex cells (gametes). There is a mixing of genetic information so the offspring show variation.
- Asexual reproduction does not involve the fusion of sex cells. All of the genetic information comes from one parent. All of the offspring are identical to the parent.
- These identical individuals are known as clones.

Key words: sexual, asexual, clone, variation

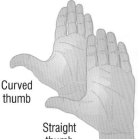

Unattached ear lobe | Attached ear lobe | Curved thumb | Straight thumb | Dimples | No dimples

These are all human characteristics which are controlled by a single pair of genes, so they can be very useful in helping us to understand how sexual reproduction introduces variety and how inheritance works

CHECK YOURSELF

1 Which type of reproduction results in variation?

2 Why does this variation arise?

3 What are identical offspring from one parent called?

B1b 6.3 Cloning

Clones are identical to the parent. Cloning is used to produce new individuals that you want.

- In plants the process is cheap and effective. Plants can be cloned by taking cuttings and growing them, or taking groups of cells and growing them under special conditions (tissue culture).
- With animals it is much more difficult to clone. Embryo transplants are used to clone animals. In this process, embryos are split into smaller groups of cells then each group is allowed to develop in a host animal.

Key words: clone, cutting, tissue culture, embryo transplant, host

CHECK YOURSELF

1 What two types of cloning are commonly used for plants?

2 When using embryo transplants the new individuals are all the same. Why are they all genetically identical?

3 What do we mean by a 'host' animal?

B1b 6.4 New ways of cloning animals

- Fusion cell and adult cell cloning are also used to clone animals.
- In adult cell cloning, the nucleus of the animal you want is placed in an empty cell. This cell is then developed in a different animal.

Key words: fusion cell cloning, adult cell cloning

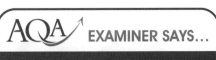

Sheep A — Adult udder cell — Nucleus removed

Mild electric shock

Nucleus from sheep A fuses with empty egg from sheep B and starts to divide to form an embryo

The cloned embryo is implanted into the uterus of sheep C

Lamb born is clone of sheep A

Sheep B — Mature egg cell — Empty egg cell

Adult cell or reproductive cloning is still a very difficult technique – but it holds out the promise of many benefits in the future.

CHECK YOURSELF

1 Look at the diagram above. What type of cell does the nucleus in the fused cell come from?

2 What type of cell provides the empty cell in the process above?

3 What is done to the fused cell to start off the process of cell division in adult cell cloning?

B1b 6.5 Genetic engineering

EXAM HINTS

It is the gene that controls how an organism develops. If you place a gene in a new organism it will develop that characteristic.

CHECK YOURSELF

1 How is a gene 'cut out' of a chromosome?

2 When a gene is inserted into a new organism, how is the new organism affected?

3 Why is genetic engineering being developed?

Genetic engineering involves changing the genetic make-up of an organism.

Genes are 'cut out' of the chromosome of an organism using an enzyme. The genes are then placed in the chromosome of another organism.

The genes may be placed in an organism of the same species so that it has 'desired' characteristics or in a different species. For example, the gene to produce insulin in humans can be placed in bacteria so that they produce insulin.

Many people argue about whether or not genetic engineering is 'right'. Will it create new organisms that we know nothing about? Is it going against nature?

Key words: enzyme, gene, desired

Human cell with insulin gene in its DNA

Bacterium with ring of DNA called a plasmid

Insulin gene cut out of DNA by an enzyme

Plasmid taken out of bacterium and split open by an enzyme

Insulin gene inserted into plasmid by another enzyme

Plasmid with insulin gene in it taken up by bacterium

Bacterium multiplies many times

The insulin gene is switched on and the insulin is harvested

Insulin

The principles of genetic engineering. A bacterial cell receives a gene from a human being.

B1b 6 End of chapter questions

1 Why is cloning plants important?

2 Why does sexual reproduction result in variation?

3 There are three methods of cloning animals. What are they?

4 What is 'tissue culture'?

5 What is present in the sex cells that result in the characteristics of the parents being passed on to the offspring?

6 Why does asexual reproduction result in offspring showing no variation?

7 If a grower wants to grow lots of plants that are identical, should he/she use cuttings or tissue culture? Explain your answer.

8 Some bacteria have been genetically engineered to produce a human hormone. What is the name of the hormone?

Pre Test: Evolution

1. What does the term 'natural selection' mean?

2. What was Lamarck's theory of evolution?

3. Why do most people not believe in Lamarck's theory now?

4. Why did it take so long for Darwin's theory to be accepted?

5. How do fossils provide evidence supporting Darwin's theory of evolution?

6. How long ago did life-forms appear on Earth?

7. In Darwin's theory of evolution, which organisms in a species are the ones that breed?

8. How do these successful members of a species pass on their characteristics to the next generation?

9. What is meant by the word 'extinction'?

10. What is meant by a 'mutation'?

---

students' book page 108

B1b 7.1 The origins of life on Earth

KEY POINTS

1. We are unsure of when life began on Earth. No one was about!
2. However fossils help us to decide when life began, although it is proving very difficult to find any really good evidence.

AQA EXAMINER SAYS...

Remember in an exam question to link fossils with rocks. They are found in different layers. This means we can put an approximate date on when different animals and plants existed.

It is believed that the Earth is about 4500 million years old and that life began about 3500 million years ago.

There is some debate as to whether the first life developed due to the conditions on Earth, or whether simple life-forms arrived from another planet.

We can date rocks. Fossils are found in rocks, so we can date when different organisms existed.

Key words: fossils, evidence

CHECK YOURSELF

1. When do we think that the first life appeared on our planet?
2. Why can we not be sure where this life came from?
3. How are fossils dated?

This amazing fossil shows two dinosaurs – prehistoric animals which died out millions of years before we appeared on Earth. Fossils can only give us a brief glimpse into the past. We will never know exactly what disaster snuffed out the life of this spectacular reptile all those years ago.

B1b 7.2 Theories of evolution

KEY POINTS

1 There are two main theories of evolution. They are those of Lamarck and Darwin.
2 Much evidence now points to the theory of Darwin being the correct one.

AQA EXAMINER SAYS...

In exams many students forget that the members of a species that survive *go on to breed*. This means their genes are passed on. Make sure that you don't forget to write this and therefore miss out on a couple of marks.

Lamarck's theory stated that acquired characteristics can be passed on to the next generation. People found this difficult to believe. For example, if two parents were to build up their muscles in the gym, Lamarck's theory would predict that this characteristic would be passed on to their offspring!

Darwin's theory stated that small changes took place over time. All organisms vary and therefore some are more likely to survive (natural selection). Those that are best adapted breed and pass on their characteristics.

It took a long time for Darwin's theory to be accepted. Many people wanted to believe that God was responsible for the creation of new species.

Key words: acquired, natural selection

In Lamarck's model of evolution, giraffes have long necks because each generation stretched up to reach the highest leaves. So each new generation had a slightly longer neck!

CHECK YOURSELF

1 What did Lamarck mean by an 'acquired characteristic'?

2 Why is it that only some organisms of a species survive to breed?

3 Why did it take so long for people to believe in Darwin's theory?

Natural selection

KEY POINTS

1 Organisms of a species all vary from one another.
2 Some organisms are more likely to survive and breed as they have 'better' characteristics. This is known as 'natural selection'.

AQA EXAMINER SAYS...

Remember that organisms are adapted in many different ways. Survival of the fittest does not mean just the fastest. It might mean those able to find food best, fight off disease, survive a 'cold snap' in the weather, etc.

Due to sexual reproduction, there is variation between members of a species. For example, all antelope are different to each other. Those members of a species with the 'best' characteristics survive to breed.

Weaker members of the species may die from:

● disease
● lack of food (or being caught by predators) or
● variation in the climate (a very wet or very cold / hot period of weather).

The survival of organisms with the 'best' characteristics is known as 'survival of the fittest'.

The fact that the best adapted animals and plants survive is known as 'natural selection'.

Key words: characteristics, 'fittest'

Rabbits with the best all-round eyesight, the sharpest hearing and the longest legs will be the ones most likely to escape being eaten by a fox

CHECK YOURSELF

1 Why is there variation between members of the same species?

2 What is meant by the phrase 'survival of the fittest'?

3 What is meant by 'natural selection'?

Extinction

AQA↗ EXAMINER SAYS...

Make sure when answering a question about extinction that you always remember to use the word 'change'. If there is no change, then species do not become extinct.

'Extinction' means that a species that once existed has been completely wiped out.

Extinction can be caused by a number of factors, but always involves a change in circumstances:

- A new disease may kill all members of a species.
- Climate change may make it too cold or hot, or wet or dry, for a species and reduce its food supply.
- A new predator may evolve or be introduced to an area that effectively kills and eats all of the species.
- A new competitor may evolve or be introduced into an area. The original species may be left with too little to eat.
- The habitat the species lives in may be destroyed.

Key words: change, disease, predator, competitor, climate change

The dinosaurs ruled the Earth for millions of years, but when the whole environment changed, they could not adapt and died out. By the time things began to warm up again, mammals, which could control their own body temperature, were becoming dominant. The age of reptiles was over.

CHECK YOURSELF

1 What does the word 'extinct' mean?

2 How might a new competitor cause the extinction of a species?

3 Give two ways that people have caused the extinction of some species.

B1b 7 — End of chapter questions

1 **What is Lamarck's theory as to how new species evolve?**

2 **What, briefly, are the two theories about how life started on Earth?**

3 **Give two reasons why a species could become extinct.**

4 **How do we know when different species lived on the Earth?**

5 **How old do we believe the Earth to be?**

6 **What is meant by the term 'survival of the fittest'?**

7 **How might a new predator arrive on an island?**

8 **Suggest two environmental conditions in an area that, if they changed, could cause problems for the animals that live there.**

1. What is meant by the term 'non-renewable'?

2. Give two ways that humans reduce the land available for animals.

3. How do humans pollute water supplies?

4. What is a fertiliser?

5. Which gas is the main cause of acid rain?

6. What is a pesticide?

7. What organisms are used as water pollution indicators?

8. Give two gases that contribute to the 'greenhouse effect'.

9. How do forests help to reduce the carbon dioxide level in the atmosphere?

10. What do we mean by 'sustainable development'?

---

students' book page 120

B1b 8.1   The effects of the population explosion

KEY POINT

The human population is increasing rapidly. So we use up more resources and produce more waste and pollution.

There are increasing numbers of people on our planet.

Many people want and demand a better standard of living.

We are using up raw materials and those that are non-renewable cannot be replaced.

We are producing more waste and the pollution that goes with it.

We are also using land that animals and plants need to live on. It is being used for building, quarrying, farming and dumping waste.

We pollute:

- the water with sewage, fertiliser and toxic chemicals
- the air with gases such as sulfur dioxide and with smoke
- the land with pesticides and herbicides and these can then be washed into the water.

The Earth from space. As the human population of the Earth grows, our impact on the planet gets bigger every day.

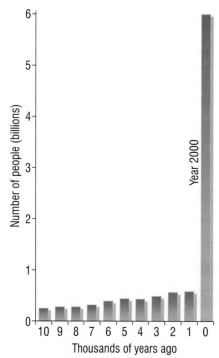

This record of human population growth shows the massive increase during the last few hundred years

---

CHECK YOURSELF

1 What are the four ways that humans use up land?

2 What are the two chemicals we pollute the land with called?

3 What word do we use to describe raw materials that cannot be replaced?

B1b 8.2 **Acid rain**

KEY POINTS

1 Sulfur dioxide is mostly responsible for acid rain.

2 Clouds blow across countries, so those producing acid rain often cause problems for somebody else!

- Burning fuels can produce sulfur dioxide (and nitrogen oxides).
- These dissolve in water in the air, forming acidic solutions.
- The solutions then fall as acid rain – sometimes a long way from where the gases were produced.
- Acid rain kills organisms. Enzymes, which control reactions, are very sensitive to pH (acidity or alkalinity).

Key words: acid, dissolve, enzymes

GET IT RIGHT!

Remember the acidity does not dissolve the organism. Living things are killed as their *enzymes* only work in a narrow range of acidity / alkalinity (pH).

CHECK YOURSELF

1 What are the main gases that cause acid rain?

2 Why does acid rain often fall a great distance from where it was produced?

3 Why do some organisms die because of acid rain?

B1b 8.3 Global warming

KEY POINTS

1 It is now widely believed that the atmosphere on the planet is warming up due to our activities.

2 It is also agreed we should do something about it. Not everyone agrees what!

- Burning fuels (combustion) releases carbon dioxide.
- Cows and rice fields release methane gas.
- Both of these gases are 'greenhouse gases'. As these gases increase in the atmosphere, it retains more heat from the Sun. The Earth is therefore warming up.
- This warming may cause a number of changes in the Earth's climate and cause sea levels to rise.
- We are cutting down forests (deforestation). This is making the problem worse because trees take up carbon dioxide (during photosynthesis). When the trees die, they release this carbon dioxide back to the atmosphere.

AQA EXAMINER SAYS...

Remember methane is also a greenhouse gas. Many students in exam answers only mention carbon dioxide. However, never mention the ozone layer – it has nothing to do with it!

Many scientists believe that this simple warming effect could, if it is not controlled, change life on Earth as we know it

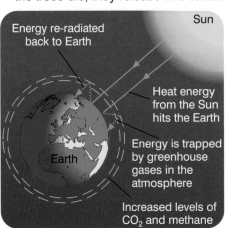

Energy re-radiated back to Earth

Sun

Heat energy from the Sun hits the Earth

Earth

Energy is trapped by greenhouse gases in the atmosphere

Increased levels of CO_2 and methane

Key words: combustion, carbon dioxide, methane, deforestation

CHECK YOURSELF

1 Where is methane produced?

2 Why does more methane and carbon dioxide in the atmosphere mean that it will heat up?

3 Why does deforestation make the problem worse?

B1b 8.4 Sustainable development

KEY POINT

If we continue to use up the Earth's resources they will run out. What then?

Sustainable woodlands have become an important and attractive part of sustainable development in the UK

As our population rises, we use up more of the Earth's resources. There are many examples, e.g. land, fossil fuels and minerals.

'Sustainable development' means finding ways of reducing this need for more resources.

This may mean finding alternatives to some resources. For example:

- fuels for cars
- recycling what we already have, e.g. plastics, aluminium in cans
- using land that has already been used previously, e.g. for building new homes.

Key words: sustainable, recycle, alternatives

AQA EXAMINER SAYS...

There are many examples here. In an exam question, you will be asked to express your views on sustainable development and why it is necessary. You will be able to use any examples that you can think of or are interested in. Make sure that you have a point of view!

CHECK YOURSELF

1 Why will we need to find alternative fuels for cars, lorries, and aeroplanes?

2 Why is it important that we re-use land?

3 Why do you think we should recycle aluminium cans?

Planning for the future

KEY POINTS

1 Lichens are indicators of the level of pollution in the air. Freshwater invertebrates are indicators of pollution in freshwater.

2 In the development of new housing for increases in the population it is important to use, as fully as possible, areas that have already been used for building and redevelop them. This helps in making development sustainable.

AQA EXAMINER SAYS...

Make sure that you remember the two indicators of pollution. Lichens for air pollution and freshwater invertebrates for water pollution.

- Lichens indicate the level of air pollution. The more species of lichen growing, the cleaner the air.
  Freshwater invertebrates indicate the level of water pollution in the same way. The wider the range of these invertebrates the cleaner the water in the streams, river or pond. Some freshwater invertebrates will only live in polluted water.

- The world population is growing and needs suitable housing. It is important not to use up green areas of the countryside too much but to use areas that have already been built upon (called brown field sites).
  Many countries put aside areas of land which are important for wildlife and will not allow any development on them.

Key words: lichen, freshwater invertebrate, pollution, sustainable

Lichens grow well where the air is clean. In a polluted area there would be far fewer species of lichen growing. This is why they are useful bio-indicators.

CHECK YOURSELF

1 Why is it important to use land previously built upon for new housing?

2 Why is it helpful that some freshwater invertebrates only live in polluted water?

3 Would you expect to find a smaller or wider range of freshwater invertebrates in clean water?

B1b 8 — End of chapter questions

1 Give two ways humans are using up more land.

2 Which organism is used as an air pollution indicator?

3 Which chemicals, in organisms, are very pH-sensitive?

4 If a tree is cut down, how might it release its carbon back to the atmosphere?

5 State two ways that humans pollute water.

6 Which gas is the main cause of the 'greenhouse effect'?

7 What are herbicides used for?

8 Name two substances that are now commonly recycled.

1 We are now able to produce animals and plants with the characteristics we want.

Match words A, B, C and D, with processes (i)–(iv) in the table.

A tissue culture
B embryo transplant
C genetic engineering
D cuttings

Process	Description
(i)	plants can be produced quickly and cheaply
(ii)	genes are transferred to another organism
(iii)	small groups of cells are taken from a plant and grown
(iv)	splitting apart cells from a fertilised egg

2 Humans affect the environment in many ways. The diagram shows some of them.

Match statements A, B, C and D, with the parts of the diagram labelled (i)–(iv).

A This place is where herbicides would be used.
B This is where most carbon dioxide is produced.
C This is where most methane is produced.
D This is where the gases that cause acid rain are produced.

3 Animals are adapted to survive the environment they live in. These drawings show four animals.

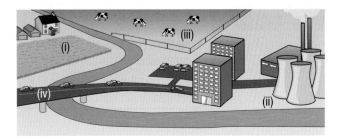

Match words A, B, C and D, with the spaces (i)–(iv) in the sentences.

A a thick layer of fat
B camouflage
C a larger surface area
D thick fur

(i) The polar bear is insulated by . . .
(ii) The seal is insulated by . . .
(iii) The Arctic fox uses its coat as . . .
(iv) The ears of the bat-eared fox give it . . .

4 Baby leopards look like their parents. This is because information is passed on to them when the sex cells from the parents fuse together.

Match words A, B, C and D, with the spaces (i)–(iv) in the sentences.

A genes   B gametes
C nucleus   D chromosomes

(i) Genetic information is passed to the young in . . .
(ii) The different characteristics are controlled by . . .
(iii) The thread-like structures that carry the information for many characteristics are called . . .
(iv) The part of the cell that carried this genetic information is the . . .

5 Humans produce many substances that cause damage to the environment.

Match words A, B, C and D, with spaces (i)–(iv) in the sentences.

A pesticides   B sulfur dioxide
C fertiliser   D methane

(i) Farmers use . . . to help their crops grow.
(ii) The gas given off by rice fields is . . .
(iii) The main gas that causes acid rain is . . .
(iv) Toxic chemicals called . . . are used to kill insects.

6 Darwins' theory of evolution was based on the theory of natural selection.

Match words A, B, C and D, with spaces (i)–(iv) in the sentences below.

A evolution   B variation
C weakness   D sexual reproduction

(i) . . . is present in a species due to (ii) . . . . This means that any member of the species showing a form of (iii) . . . is not likely to breed. This is known as 'survival of the fittest' and results in (iv) . . . .

 Test & Assessment Interactive quizzes, answers and hints online!

7 It is now possible to clone cats. This means that if your pet cat dies you can create an identical copy. It is a difficult and expensive process. The diagram below shows how it can be done.

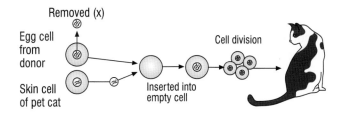

(i) The process shown above is:
  A   sexual reproduction
  B   fertilisation
  C   asexual reproduction
  D   fusion

(ii) What is removed from the egg cell of the donor cat (X)?
  A   cytoplasm   B   DNA
  C   nutrients   D   membrane

(iii) The new cat is a clone of the original pet as they have the:
  A   same colour   B   same enzymes
  C   same cells   D   same genes

(iv) Many people object to animal cloning. For what reason do most people object?
  A   It costs a lot.
  B   It is not morally right.
  C   It hurts the animal.
  D   It cannot be available to everyone.

8 Scientists use lichens as indicators of air pollution. Studies are carried out to find out how many species of lichen live in certain areas. Here are some results.

Distance from a city centre (km)	Number of species of lichen found
0	2
1	3
2	8
3	9
4	15
5	18
6	27

(i) The air with the least pollution is found:
  A   in the city centre
  B   2 km from the centre
  C   4 km from the centre
  D   5 km from the centre

(ii) What is the relationship, if any, between the distance from the city centre and the number of different lichen species found?
  A   It is directly proportional.
  B   It is indirectly proportional.
  C   There is no relationship.
  D   There is a relationship.

(iii) The gas responsible for the pollution that the lichens are sensitive to, is:
  A   sulfur dioxide
  B   carbon dioxide
  C   nitrogen
  D   methane

(iv) The organisms that are used as indicators of pollution in rivers and ponds are:
  A   vertebrate animals
  B   freshwater fish
  C   freshwater plants
  D   invertebrate animals

9 Most scientists now accept Darwin's theory of evolution.

(i) Darwin's theory states that all living organisms have evolved from:
  A   substances present in the atmosphere
  B   chemicals present in the earth
  C   simple living things
  D   dead or inactive organisms

(ii) It is thought that the first living organisms were present on the Earth:
  A   500 million years ago
  B   1500 million years ago
  C   3500 million years ago
  D   4500 million years ago

(iii) We cannot know how life on Earth began as:
  A   there is no evidence
  B   it is so long ago
  C   there are still religious arguments
  D   only plants existed at the time

(iv) Dinosaurs became extinct a very long time ago. We think that the most likely reason for them becoming extinct is:
  A   they were too successful
  B   they faced competition from other animals
  C   they caught a disease that they were not immune to
  D   the conditions on Earth changed

C1a | Products from rocks

Checklist

This spider diagram shows the topics in the unit. You can copy it out and add your notes and questions around it, or cross off each section when you feel confident you know it for your exams.

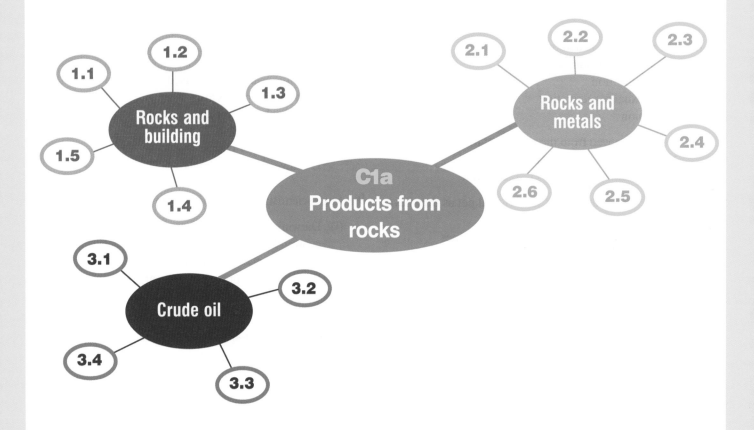

Tick when you:

reviewed it after your lesson	☑	☐	☐
revised once – some questions right	☑	☑	☐
revised twice – all questions right	☑	☑	☑

Move on to another topic when you have all three ticks.

Chapter 1 Rocks and building

1.1	Atoms, elements and compounds	☐	☐	☐
1.2	Limestone and its uses	☐	☐	☐
1.3	Decomposing carbonates	☐	☐	☐
1.4	Quicklime and slaked lime	☐	☐	☐
1.5	Cement, concrete and glass	☐	☐	☐

Chapter 2 Rocks and metals

2.1	Extracting metals	☐	☐	☐
2.2	Extracting iron	☐	☐	☐
2.3	Properties of iron and steels	☐	☐	☐
2.4	Alloys in everyday use	☐	☐	☐
2.5	Transition metals	☐	☐	☐
2.6	Aluminium and titanium	☐	☐	☐

Chapter 3 Crude oil

3.1	Fuels from crude oil	☐	☐	☐
3.2	Fractional distillation	☐	☐	☐
3.3	Burning fuels	☐	☐	☐
3.4	Cleaner fuels	☐	☐	☐

What are you expected to know?

Chapter 1 Rocks and building (See students' book pages 138–149)

- All substances are made of atoms that have a tiny central nucleus surrounded by electrons.
- The simplest substances contain only one type of atom and are called 'elements'.
- Atoms of each element have their own chemical symbol.
- The periodic table lists all the known elements in groups with similar chemical properties.
- Elements form compounds by combining with other elements: their atoms give, take or share electrons, so they bond together.
- The formula of a substance shows the types of atom it contains and how many have combined together.
- In chemical reactions, the mass of the reactants is always the same as the mass of the products.
- Chemical equations are balanced. There is the same number of each type of atom on each side.
- Limestone is used as a building material and to make quicklime, slaked lime, cement and glass.
- Heating metal carbonates produces metal oxides and carbon dioxide gas.

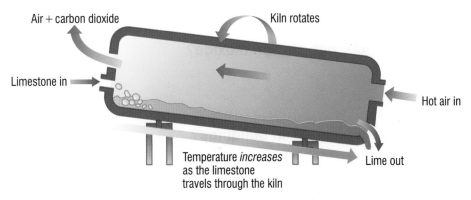

Air + carbon dioxide

Kiln rotates

Limestone in

Hot air in

Temperature *increases*
as the limestone
travels through the kiln

Lime out

A rotary lime kiln

Chapter 2 Rocks and metals (See students' book pages 152–165)

- We get metals from ores that are dug from the Earth.
- Most metals have to be extracted from their ores using chemical reactions, and this can use large amounts of energy.
- A metal mixed with other elements is called an alloy.
- Alloys have different properties to pure metals and can be designed for specific uses.
- Iron, copper, gold, aluminium, titanium and their alloys have many uses.
- Recycling, and new ways of extracting metals, helps to conserve energy and resources.

Chapter 3 Crude oil (See students' book pages 168–177)

- Crude oil is a mixture of many different hydrocarbons.
- Alkanes are saturated hydrocarbons with the general formula C_nH_{2n+2}
- Fractional distillation separates crude oil into fractions, many of which are used as fuels.
- Burning fuels pollutes the atmosphere with carbon dioxide, sulfur dioxide and particulates.
- Producing cleaner and better fuels can help reduce pollution.

1. Is the substance represented by the formula CH_4 an element or a compound?

2. What happens to atoms in chemical reactions?

3. What are the main uses of limestone?

4. What are the products when limestone is heated strongly?

5. Which metal carbonates decompose on heating?

6. Write a balanced equation for the thermal decomposition of magnesium carbonate.

7. How is slaked lime made?

8. What happens when slaked lime reacts with carbon dioxide?

9. How is concrete made?

10. What are the two main reasons for using glass in buildings?

---

students' book page 138

C1a 1.1 Atoms, elements and compounds

KEY POINTS

1. All substances are made of atoms.
2. Elements are substances made of only one type of atom.
3. Symbols are used for atoms to show what happens in chemical reactions.

- There are about 100 different elements from which all substances are made.
- Elements are listed in the periodic table.
- Each element is made of one type of atom.
- Atoms are represented by a chemical symbol, e.g. Na for an atom of sodium, O for an atom of oxygen.
- Atoms have a tiny nucleus surrounded by electrons. When elements react their atoms join with atoms of other elements.
- Atoms form chemical bonds by losing, gaining or sharing a small number of electrons.
- Compounds contain two or more elements bonded together.

Key words: atom, compound, electron, element, symbol

AQA EXAMINER SAYS...

Remember that a symbol represents one atom of an element.

CHECK YOURSELF

1. What substances are made of only one type of atom?

2. What do symbols represent?

3. What is a compound?

Electrons

Nucleus

Atoms consist of a small nucleus surrounded by electrons

C1a 1.2 Limestone and its uses

We quarry large amounts of limestone rock because it has many uses.

Blocks of limestone can be used for building, and it is used to make:

- quicklime
- cement
- glass.

Limestone is made up mainly of calcium carbonate, formula $CaCO_3$.

When heated strongly, calcium carbonate decomposes to make quicklime (calcium oxide, CaO) and carbon dioxide (CO_2).

We can represent the reaction by the word equation:

calcium carbonate → calcium oxide + carbon dioxide

This is done on a large scale in lime kilns.

Key words: formula, quicklime, thermal decomposition, word equation

KEY POINTS

1. Limestone is used as a building material and to make quicklime, cement and glass.
2. Thermal decomposition of limestone makes quicklime and carbon dioxide.
3. The formula of a substance shows the number of atoms of each element that have joined together.

GET IT RIGHT!

Thermal decomposition means 'breaking down using heat': you need to make both points to get full marks.

CHECK YOURSELF

1. Give four uses of limestone.
2. What do we mean by 'thermal decomposition'?
3. How many different elements are there in calcium carbonate, $CaCO_3$?
4. How many atoms are there in the formula of calcium carbonate, $CaCO_3$?

C1a 1.3 Decomposing carbonates

Metal carbonates decompose in a similar way to calcium carbonate when heated strongly enough.

A Bunsen burner flame is not hot enough to decompose sodium carbonate or potassium carbonate.

The reactions can be represented by balanced chemical equations. For example:

$$CaCO_3 \rightarrow CaO + CO_2$$

- Symbol equations should be balanced with the same number of each type of atom on both sides.
- Atoms are not created or destroyed in chemical reactions. So the mass of the products is always the same as the mass of the reactants.

Key words: balanced chemical equation

KEY POINTS

1. Carbonates of metals decompose when heated to produce the metal oxide and carbon dioxide.
2. We can represent chemical reactions by balanced equations.
3. In a chemical reaction the mass of the reactants is equal to the mass of the products.

BUMP UP YOUR GRADE

For grade B and above: make sure you can write balanced symbol equations as well as word equations for all the reactions in this section.

 EXAMINER SAYS...

You should be able to write equations for the decomposition of any metal carbonate.

CHECK YOURSELF

1. Name the products when zinc carbonate is thermally decomposed.
2. Name two carbonates that do not decompose when heated with a Bunsen burner.
3. Write a balanced chemical equation for the thermal decomposition of copper(II) carbonate.
4. 10.0 g of magnesium carbonate was heated strongly. What mass of products would be formed?

C1a 1.4 Quicklime and slaked lime

KEY POINTS

1 Adding water to quicklime produces slaked lime.
2 Lime water is used as a test for carbon dioxide.
3 Mortar can be made by mixing slaked lime, sand and water.

AQA EXAMINER SAYS...

Make sure you can write equations for the reactions of quicklime with water and slaked lime with carbon dioxide.

EXAM HINTS

Make sure you check that any equations you write are correctly balanced – count the atoms on both sides.

- Quicklime (calcium oxide) reacts with water to produce slaked lime (calcium hydroxide).
- Calcium hydroxide is only slightly soluble in water, but a little dissolves to form a solution called lime water.
- Calcium hydroxide reacts with carbon dioxide to form calcium carbonate, which is insoluble in water. This is why carbon dioxide bubbled into lime water makes it go cloudy.
- Mortar is used to hold stone or bricks together in buildings. Lime mortar is made by mixing slaked lime mixed with sand and adding water.
- When carbon dioxide in the air reacts with the calcium hydroxide in the mortar it forms calcium carbonate and sets hard.

Key words: lime water, mortar, slaked lime

Lime mortar should be used to repair old buildings

CHECK YOURSELF

1 Write the word equation for the reaction of carbon dioxide with calcium hydroxide.

2 Write the balanced chemical equation for carbon dioxide reacting with lime water.

3 Why does carbon dioxide turn lime water milky?

4 Why does lime mortar set hard?

C1a 1.5 Cement, concrete and glass

KEY POINTS

1 Cement is made by heating a mixture of limestone and clay.
2 Concrete is made by mixing cement with sand, stones or crushed rock and water.
3 Glass can be made from limestone, sand and sodium carbonate.

- To make cement, limestone is mixed with clay, heated strongly and the product is powdered.
- Mortar made with cement and sand is stronger and sets faster than lime mortar. It will set in wet conditions, even under water.
- A mixture of cement, sand, stones or crushed rock and water is called 'concrete'. This can be poured into moulds or spread out before it sets to produce different shapes. Concrete can be reinforced by pouring it around steel.
- Glass is used to allow light into buildings and make them weatherproof. The properties of these materials can be modified for specific uses. This can be done by using different proportions of the main ingredients or by adding other substances.

Key words: cement, concrete, glass

GET IT RIGHT!

Make sure you know the differences between cement, mortar and concrete.

CHECK YOURSELF

1 Why is cement mortar more useful than lime mortar?
2 What is concrete?
3 How can concrete be made even stronger?
4 Why is glass so useful in buildings?

Glass can produce some spectacular buildings

C1a 1 End of chapter questions

1 Which of these substances are compounds? Ca, Cl_2, CO_2, $MgCO_3$, O_2

2 How do atoms join together in a compound?

3 Give four uses of limestone.

4 Write a word equation for the thermal decomposition of calcium carbonate.

5 Why is the mass of the products of a chemical reaction always the same as the mass of reactants?

6 Name a metal carbonate that does not decompose when heated with a Bunsen burner flame.

7 Write a balanced equation for the reaction of calcium hydroxide with carbon dioxide.

8 How is lime mortar made?

9 How is cement made?

10 Suggest two methods that could be used when making glass to change its properties.

Pre Test: Rocks and metals

1. What is an ore?
2. What chemical reactions do we use to extract metals?
3. How is iron extracted?
4. What is cast iron?
5. Why is pure iron soft and easily bent?
6. What are the main types of steel?
7. What are alloys?
8. What are 'smart' alloys?
9. What are the properties of transition metals?
10. How is copper produced?
11. What two properties of aluminium and titanium make them especially useful metals?
12. Why is it expensive to extract aluminium and titanium?

---

students' book page 152 C1a 2.1 **Extracting metals**

KEY POINTS

1. An ore contains enough metal to make it worth extracting the metal.
2. The method we use to extract a metal depends on its reactivity.
3. Many metals can be extracted from their oxides using carbon.

Rocks that contain enough of a metal or a metal compound to make it worth extracting the metal are called 'ores'.

A few very unreactive metals like gold are found native as the metal. Gold can be separated from rocks by physical methods. However, most metals are found as compounds and so have to be extracted by chemical reactions.

- Metals can be extracted from compounds by displacement using a more reactive element or by electrolysis.
- Metals that are less reactive than carbon can be extracted by heating with carbon to reduce their oxides. (Reduction is the removal of oxygen from a compound.) This method is used commercially if possible.

Key words: displacement, electrolysis, ore, native, reduce

CHECK YOURSELF

1. What are ores?
2. What is meant by the term 'native metal'?
3. Name two metals that can be extracted by reduction with carbon.
4. Name a metal that is too reactive to be extracted using carbon.
5. What happens in a reduction reaction?

C1a 2.2 Extracting iron

KEY POINTS

1 Iron ore contains iron oxide.
2 Iron oxide is reduced in a blast furnace using coke.
3 The iron that is produced is hard and brittle because it contains impurities.

AQA EXAMINER SAYS...

You do not need to remember technical details of the blast furnace.

Many of the ores used to produce iron contain iron(III) oxide.
Iron is less reactive than carbon and so it can be extracted from its ore using carbon.

Iron is extracted in a blast furnace using coke to provide the carbon. The iron oxide is reduced at high temperatures by the carbon.

The iron produced contains about 4% impurities that make it hard and brittle. Its properties mean that it has only a small number of uses as cast iron. However, it is the starting material for making steels.

Key words: coke, reduced, cast iron

CHECK YOURSELF

1 Name the compound of iron that is reduced in the blast furnace.

2 What substance provides the carbon in the blast furnace?

3 Write a word equation for a reaction that produces iron in the blast furnace.

4 Why is cast iron only useful as a metal for some purposes?

C1a 2.3 Properties of iron and steels

KEY POINTS

1 Pure iron is a soft metal that bends easily.
2 Steels are alloys of iron.
3 There are many different steels that have properties suitable for particular uses.

AQA EXAMINER SAYS...

Make sure you know the three main types of steel and what they contain.

- **Pure iron** has a regular arrangement of atoms. The atoms are in layers that slide easily over each other so its shape can be easily changed.
- **Steels** are alloys of iron – they are mixtures that contain other elements as well as iron. The other elements change the regular structure of the metal and this changes its properties.
- **Carbon steels** contain small amounts of carbon, up to 1.5%. Increasing the amount of carbon in a steel makes it harder but more brittle.
- **Low-alloy steels** contain up to 5% of other metals to give them special properties.
- **High-alloy steels** contain higher percentages of other metals, e.g. stainless steel contains about 25% chromium and nickel, and it does not rust.

Key words: alloy, carbon steels, low-alloy steels, high-alloy steels

CHECK YOURSELF

1 Why is pure iron soft?

2 What are steels?

3 What is the maximum percentage of carbon in carbon steels?

4 A tall television transmitter mast is made of steel that contains 2% manganese. What type of steel is it?

Iron

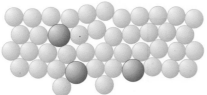

Alloy

The atoms in pure iron are arranged in layers which can easily slide over one another. In alloys the layers cannot slide so easily because atoms of other elements change the regular structure.

C1a 2.4 Alloys in everyday use

KEY POINTS

1 A pure metal is alloyed by mixing it with other metals or elements.
2 Alloying changes the properties of a pure metal so that it is more useful.
3 Smart alloys have special properties such as returning to their original shape.

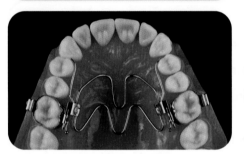

This dental brace pulls the teeth into the right position as it warms up. That's smart!

- Many pure metals are too soft and lose their shape too easily. Mixing a pure metal with other metals or elements to make an alloy makes the metal harder.
- Alloying may also affect other properties of the metal, such as strength, appearance and resistance to corrosion. The cost of an alloy depends on the cost of the metals it contains.
- Alloys are mixtures. This means that the amounts of the elements they contain can be varied so they can be designed with specific properties for a particular use.
- Shape memory alloys are 'smart' because they return to their original shape after they have been bent.

Key words: alloy, mixture, shape memory alloys

 EXAMINER SAYS...

When asked for properties, many students include cost or cheapness but cost is not a property of a substance.

CHECK YOURSELF

1 List four properties of a metal that can be changed by alloying.

2 Why can the amounts of the elements in an alloy be varied?

3 Why are some alloys 'smart'?

C1a 2.5 Transition metals

KEY POINTS

1 Transition metals have many similar properties that make them very useful.
2 Copper is a very good conductor of heat and electricity that does not corrode easily.
3 Extracting copper by traditional methods is expensive and affects the environment.

The elements between Groups 2 and 3 in the periodic table are all metals and are called the 'transition metals'.

- They are good conductors of heat and electricity.
- They are strong, hard and dense, but can be bent or hammered into shape.
- Except for mercury, transition metals have high melting points.

Transition metals have many similar properties but there are differences that make them useful for specific purposes.

Copper is particularly useful for plumbing and electrical wires. Copper is processed by smelting and electrolysis.

Little high-grade copper ore remains, and so huge amounts of rock have to be moved in open cast mines. New methods of extracting copper are being developed, including using bacteria, fungi and plants.

Key words: transition metals, smelting, electrolysis

CHECK YOURSELF

1 Where in the periodic table are the transition elements?

2 In what ways are the transition elements similar?

3 Why are new methods to extract copper being developed?

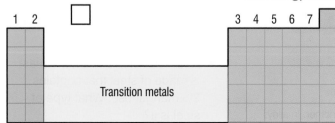

The transition metals

C1a 2.6 Aluminium and titanium

KEY POINTS

1 Aluminium and titanium have low densities compared with many other metals.
2 They also resist corrosion, and titanium is strong at high temperatures.
3 Extracting these metals is expensive because it involves electrolysis and high temperatures.
4 Recycling saves resources and the energy needed to extract the metal from its ore.

AQA EXAMINER SAYS...

As well as knowing the similarities between aluminium and titanium, make sure you know the differences.

We use aluminium and titanium where low density and resistance to corrosion are important. Both metals form oxide layers that protect them from further corrosion.

- Aluminium is soft with quite a low melting point but can be hardened by alloying.
- Titanium reacts with carbon and so is extracted by displacement with a reactive metal e.g. sodium.
- Aluminium and sodium are too reactive to extract with carbon and so electrolysis is used, with high costs for energy.
- Aluminium is widely used in buildings, cans, cooking foil, electricity cables and aircraft.
- Titanium is used in jet engines, nuclear reactors, replacement hip joints and bicycles.

Recycling metals avoids mining and processing metal ores.

Key words: displacement, oxide layers, recycling

GET IT RIGHT!

Aluminium is a reactive metal, near to the top of the reactivity series.

However, it is protected by a tough layer of oxide on its surface.

CHECK YOURSELF

1 What properties make aluminium and titanium especially useful metals?
2 Why is titanium extracted by displacement using a very reactive metal?
3 Why is aluminium extracted using electrolysis?
4 What are the benefits of recycling metals?

C1a 2 End of chapter questions

1 **How much metal or metal compound is in an ore?**

2 **Suggest how zinc would be extracted from zinc oxide commercially.**

3 **Why does the reaction to produce iron involve reduction?**

4 **Why is cast iron brittle?**

5 **Name two elements in all carbon steels.**

6 **What is meant by 'high-alloy steels'?**

7 **Why are many metals used as alloys?**

8 **What type of alloys return to their original shape?**

9 **All transition metals conduct heat and electricity. Give one other property of all transition metals (except mercury).**

10 **Give one advantage of using bacteria or fungi to help extract copper.**

11 **What protects aluminium and tin from corrosion?**

12 **How is electrolysis involved in the extraction of titanium?**

Pre Test: Crude oil

1. What two elements make up the main compounds in crude oil?

2. What are alkanes?

3. What method is used to separate crude oil in a refinery?

4. What are fractions?

5. What are the products of burning hydrocarbons completely?

6. What other substances can be produced by burning fossil fuels?

7. What are the three main effects on the environment of burning fossil fuels?

8. How can we reduce the effects of burning fossil fuels?

---

students' book page 168 C1a 3.1

Fuels from crude oil

KEY POINTS

1 Crude oil is a mixture of many different compounds.
2 Distillation separates liquids with different boiling points.
3 Most of the compounds in crude oil are hydrocarbons, and many of these are alkanes.

Crude oil contains many different compounds that boil at different temperatures. These burn under different conditions so it needs to be separated to make useful fuels.

We can separate mixtures of liquids by distillation. Simple distillation of crude oil can produce liquids that boil within different temperature ranges.

Most of the compounds in crude oil are hydrocarbons. This means that they contain carbon and hydrogen only. Many of these hydrocarbons are alkanes, with the general formula C_nH_{2n+2}. Alkanes contain as many hydrogen atoms as possible in each molecule and so we call them saturated hydrocarbons.

Molecules can be represented by:

- a molecular formula that shows the *number* of each type of atom
- a structural formula that shows *how* the atoms are bonded together.

Key words: distillation, hydrocarbons, alkanes, molecular formula, saturated hydrocarbons, structural formula

Ethane

Propane

We can represent alkanes like this, showing all of the atoms in the molecule. The line between two atoms in the molecule is the chemical bond holding them together.

CHECK YOURSELF

1 Why does crude oil need to be separated?

2 What method can we use to separate mixtures of liquids?

3 What are hydrocarbons?

4 How can we represent molecules?

C1a 3.2 Fractional distillation

EXAM HINTS

Make sure you can explain how fractional distillation works.

GET IT RIGHT!

Small molecules – compounds with low boiling points – top of fractionating column.

Crude oil is separated at refineries by fractional distillation.

The crude oil is vaporised and fed into a fractionating column. This is a tall tower that is hot at the bottom and cooler at the top.

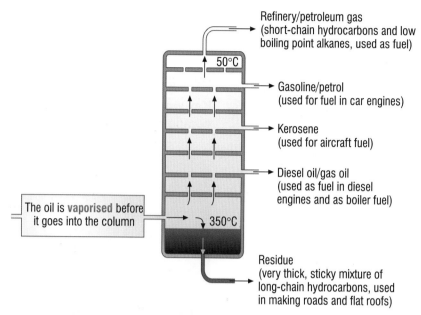

Refinery/petroleum gas (short-chain hydrocarbons and low boiling point alkanes, used as fuel)

50°C

Gasoline/petrol (used for fuel in car engines)

Kerosene (used for aircraft fuel)

The oil is **vaporised** before it goes into the column

Diesel oil/gas oil (used as fuel in diesel engines and as boiler fuel)

350°C

Residue (very thick, sticky mixture of long-chain hydrocarbons, used in making roads and flat roofs)

We use fractional distillation to turn the mixture of hydrocarbons in crude oil into fractions, each containing compounds with similar boiling points

Inside the column there are many trays with holes to allow gases through. The vapours move up the column and condense on the trays when they reach their boiling points.

There are outlets at different levels to collect the liquid fractions.

Hydrocarbons with the *smallest* molecules have the *lowest* boiling points and so are collected at the *top* of the tower. The fractions collected at the bottom have the highest boiling points.

Fractions with low boiling points burn more easily, which makes them more useful as fuels.

Key words: fractionating column, fractions

AQA EXAMINER SAYS...

Some students confuse simple distillation done in the laboratory with fractional distillation. Simple distillation is done in *steps*, but fractional distillation is a *continuous process*.

CHECK YOURSELF

1 Name the process used to separate crude oil in a refinery.

2 How does this process work?

3 What sort of hydrocarbons are in the fractions collected near the top of the column?

4 Which fractions are more difficult to burn?

C1a 3.3 Burning fuels

KEY POINTS

1 Burning hydrocarbons in plenty of air produces carbon dioxide and water.
2 In a limited supply of air, carbon monoxide and particles may be produced.
3 Any sulfur compounds in the fuel burn to produce sulfur dioxide.

When pure hydrocarbons burn completely, they produce carbon dioxide and water. However, the fuels we use are not always burnt completely and they may also contain other substances.

In a limited supply of air, such as in an engine, carbon monoxide and carbon may also be produced, and some of the hydrocarbons may not burn. Carbon and unburnt hydrocarbons form tiny particles in the air.

Most fossil fuels contain sulfur compounds. When the fuel burns these sulfur compounds produce sulfur dioxide.

Key words: carbon monoxide, unburnt hydrocarbons, particles, sulfur compounds, sulfur dioxide

The effect of many cars in a small area. Smog formed from car pollution can harm us.

BUMP UP YOUR GRADE

For grade C and above, you should be able to write balanced symbol equations for the combustion of an alkane, given its formula.

AQA EXAMINER SAYS...

You should be able to write equations for burning hydrocarbons.

CHECK YOURSELF

1 Name the products when hydrocarbons burn in plenty of air.

2 What else may be produced in a limited supply of air?

3 Why is sulfur dioxide produced when fossil fuels burn?

Cleaner fuels

KEY POINTS

1 Carbon dioxide contributes to global warming.
2 Particulates cause global dimming.
3 Sulfur dioxide forms acid rain.

AQA EXAMINER SAYS...

You should be able to link the products of burning fossil fuels with three main environmental effects. Other effects are covered in B1b, Chapter 8 'How people affect the planet'. You should also know about some developments to overcome problems with fuels.

The products from burning fossil fuels are released into the atmosphere in exhaust gases.

- Carbon dioxide is a greenhouse gas. It reduces the amount of heat lost from the Earth and causes global warming.
- Particulates cause health problems and cause global dimming by reflecting sunlight away from the Earth.
- Sulfur dioxide dissolves in water and forms acid rain. The amount of sulfur dioxide released can be reduced by removing sulfur compounds from fuels at the refinery, or by removing sulfur dioxide from the waste gases after burning.

Fossil fuel resources are being used up and will run out in the future. Plants can provide sugars to make ethanol, or can produce oils that can be used as biodiesel.

Key words: greenhouse gas, global warming, global dimming, acid rain

We can use plants that make sugar to produce ethanol by fermenting the sugar using yeast. We can then add the ethanol to petrol, making **gasohol**. Not only does this reduce the amount of oil needed, it also produces less pollution because gasohol burns more cleanly than pure petrol.

CHECK YOURSELF

1 How does burning fossil fuels cause global warming?

2 What is 'global dimming'?

3 How can we reduce the amount of sulfur dioxide released?

C1a 3   End of chapter questions

1 **Why can crude oil be separated by distillation?**

2 **What is the formula of the alkane with four carbon atoms?**

3 **What are the two main processes in fractional distillation?**

4 **Where are the fractions that burn most easily collected?**

5 **Write a word equation for the complete combustion of the hydrocarbon called propane.**

6 **What is in the particles produced by incomplete combustion of fossil fuels?**

7 **Why does burning fossil fuels contribute to global warming?**

8 **Name the element in compounds in fossil fuels that results in acid rain.**

1 The diagram shows the limestone story.

Match formulae A, B, C and D with the numbers (i)–(iv) in the flow diagram to show what happens in this process.

A $CaCO_3$
B CaO
C $Ca(OH)_2$
D CO_2

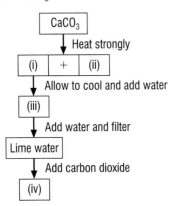

2 This question is about some groups of substances.

Match the descriptions A, B, C, D with the groups (i)–(iv) in the table.

A   all elements   B   all compounds
C   all mixtures   D   all metals

Group	Substances
(i)	bronze, calcium, copper
(ii)	calcium carbonate, carbon dioxide, water
(iii)	carbon, iron, oxygen
(iv)	concrete, mortar, steel

3 This question is about some building materials.

Match words A, B, C and D, with building materials (i)–(iv) in the table.

A   cement   B   concrete
C   glass   D   mortar

Building material	Description
(i)	a mixture of sand, stones, cement and water
(ii)	a mixture of slaked lime, sand and water
(iii)	made by heating limestone and clay
(iv)	made by heating limestone, sand and sodium carbonate

4 Match the chemical equations A, B, C and D, with descriptions (i)–(iv).

A $CaCO_3 \rightarrow CaO + CO_2$
B $Ca(OH)_2 + CO_2 \rightarrow CaCO_3 + H_2O$
C $CaO + H_2O \rightarrow Ca(OH)_2$
D $2CaO + C \rightarrow 2Ca + CO_2$

(i)   This equation represents the formation of slaked lime.
(ii) This equation represents the reaction that causes lime mortar to harden.
(iii) This reaction takes place in a lime kiln.
(iv) This reaction would not take place at any temperature.

5 The diagram shows the main steps in making steels.

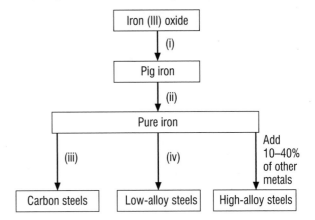

Match the statements A, B, C and D with each of the steps (i)–(iv).

A   add small amounts of carbon
B   add up to 5% of other metals
C   reduce with carbon
D   remove impurities

6 This question is about the effects of burning fuels.

Match the words A, B, C and D with the spaces (i)–(iv) in the sentences.

A   acid rain
B   global dimming
C   global warming
D   human poisoning

(i)   Burning fossil fuels in plenty of air produces carbon dioxide, which causes . . . .
(ii) If the air supply is limited carbon monoxide may be produced, which causes . . . .
(iii) This may also produce particles containing carbon and unburnt hydrocarbons, which cause . . . .
(iv) Most fossil fuels also produce sulfur dioxide, which causes . . . .

7 Crude oil can be separated in a fractionating column.

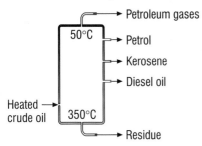

(i) Crude oil can be separated in this way because it is:
   A   a compound of carbon and hydrogen only
   B   a mixture of compounds
   C   a thick, viscous liquid
   D   broken down by heat

(ii) The crude oil is heated before it goes into the column so that it is:
   A   decomposed   B   thick and viscous
   C   thin and runny   D   vaporised

(iii) The fractions are collected at different levels because they:
   A   burn at different temperatures
   B   condense at different temperatures
   C   flow at different rates
   D   have different densities

(iv) The diesel oil fraction has molecules that:
   A   are larger than those in petrol
   B   are larger than those in the residue
   C   are smaller than those in petrol
   D   are smaller than those in petroleum gases

8 Aluminium and titanium are useful metals.

(i) Aluminium and titanium are more expensive than iron because:
   A   they both have very high melting points
   B   the energy costs to extract them are high
   C   they have more uses than iron
   D   their ores are rare

(ii) Aluminium and titanium resist corrosion because they:
   A   are both unreactive metals
   B   are both hard metals
   C   both have low densities
   D   both have oxide layers

(iii) Aluminium and titanium are used in aircraft because they:
   A   are both unreactive metals
   B   are expensive to produce
   C   both have high melting points
   D   both have low densities

(iv) Recycling aluminium is important because:
   A   there is very little aluminium ore left
   B   electrolysis is used to extract it
   C   it does not corrode
   D   it is used in so many alloys

9 Read the passage and use the information to help you answer the questions.

An open cast mine at Bingham Canyon provides over 10% of the copper used by the USA. Bingham Canyon is in mountains at the edge of the Great Salt Lake Desert. In the past, miners at Bingham Canyon dug underground mines into a mountain rich in metal ores. They were mining silver and gold and ignored the copper ore. When the gold and silver had been removed the area went into decline. A mining company found that the mountain contained large deposits of low-grade copper ore and decided to extract it using an open cast mine. Every day the mine produces 685 tonnes of copper by digging 225 000 tonnes of rock. The mountain has now been removed and replaced by a huge open pit. The waste is dumped in the canyon and in a salt lake that was used by birds and other wildlife. The mine attracted thousands of migrant workers to the area, and the mining company built new towns to replace the old temporary towns that the underground miners had put up.

(i) What is the percentage of copper in the ore according to the figures in the passage?
   A   0.1%   B   0.3%
   C   1.0%   D   3.0%

(ii) Why did the underground miners in the past ignore the copper ore?
   A   Copper was not used at that time.
   B   It was not worthwhile for them to extract the copper.
   C   There was more gold and silver.
   D   They could not dig it out of the mountain.

(iii) An open cast mine is used to extract the copper ore instead of an underground mine. This is because an open cast mine:
   A   is less unsightly
   B   moves larger amounts of rock
   C   provides better quality ore
   D   produces less waste

(iv) Which of the following is a disadvantage to the area caused by the open cast mine?
   A   More people moving into the area.
   B   Old towns replaced by modern towns.
   C   Underground mines destroyed.
   D   Wildlife habitats lost.

C1b | Oils, Earth and atmosphere

Checklist

This spider diagram shows the topics in the unit. You can copy it out and add your notes and questions around it, or cross off each section when you feel confident you know it for your exams.

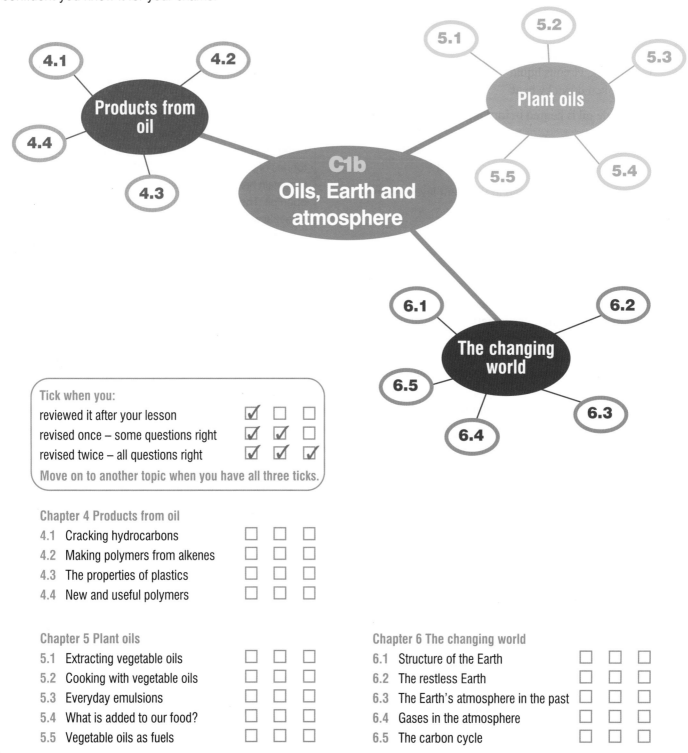

Tick when you:

reviewed it after your lesson	☑	☐	☐
revised once – some questions right	☑	☑	☐
revised twice – all questions right	☑	☑	☑

Move on to another topic when you have all three ticks.

Chapter 4 Products from oil

4.1	Cracking hydrocarbons	☐	☐	☐
4.2	Making polymers from alkenes	☐	☐	☐
4.3	The properties of plastics	☐	☐	☐
4.4	New and useful polymers	☐	☐	☐

Chapter 5 Plant oils

5.1	Extracting vegetable oils	☐	☐	☐
5.2	Cooking with vegetable oils	☐	☐	☐
5.3	Everyday emulsions	☐	☐	☐
5.4	What is added to our food?	☐	☐	☐
5.5	Vegetable oils as fuels	☐	☐	☐

Chapter 6 The changing world

6.1	Structure of the Earth	☐	☐	☐
6.2	The restless Earth	☐	☐	☐
6.3	The Earth's atmosphere in the past	☐	☐	☐
6.4	Gases in the atmosphere	☐	☐	☐
6.5	The carbon cycle	☐	☐	☐

What are you expected to know?

Chapter 4 Products from oil (*See students' book pages 184–193*)

- We use cracking to break down hydrocarbons into smaller molecules.

- The products of cracking include alkanes that are used as fuels and alkenes that can be used to make other chemicals and polymers.

- Alkenes are unsaturated with a general formula C_nH_{2n} and contain a double carbon–carbon bond.

- Alkene molecules are monomers that can add together to make polymers.

- Polymers with different properties can be made by using different starting materials and by using different reaction conditions. This allows new polymers to be developed for specific uses.

- Polymers that are not biodegradable can lead to problems with waste disposal.

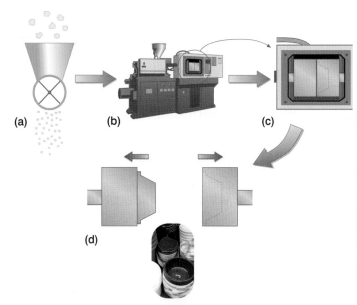

(a) (b) (c) (d)

A very common way of making things out of polymers is to use a thermosoftening plastic that can be shaped in a mould: **(a)** chunks of monomer are ground into small pieces. **(b)** These are heated to melt them and then . . . **(c)** . . . the molten plastic is forced into a mould. **(d)** The mould is separated to release the finished article.

Chapter 5 Plant oils

(*See students' book pages 196–207*)

- Vegetable oils are important as foods and fuels.

- Vegetable oils can be extracted from seeds, nuts and fruits.

- Oils do not dissolve in water, but can be mixed with water to produce emulsions that have many uses.

- Many vegetable oils are unsaturated. This can be tested using bromine or iodine.

- Unsaturated oils can be made into solids at room temperature by hydrogenation to produce saturated fats.

- Chemical analysis can be used to identify the additives that may be contained, legally or illegally, in foods.

Chapter 6 The changing world (*See students' book pages 210–223*)

- Mountains were once thought to have formed by the Earth shrinking as it cooled.

- It is now thought that movements of large parts of the Earth's crust and upper mantle, called tectonic plates, produce mountains, volcanoes and earthquakes.

- It is believed that the oceans were formed from water vapour released by volcanoes and that the Earth's early atmosphere was mainly carbon dioxide.

- Plants took up carbon dioxide by photosynthesis, and the oceans dissolved carbon dioxide; plants produced the oxygen that is now in the atmosphere.

- The atmosphere has changed little in the last 200 million years, but recently, burning fossil fuels has increased the proportion of carbon dioxide.

Pre Test: Products from oil

1. **What is cracking?**

2. **What are alkenes?**

3. **What is a polymer?**

4. **How is poly(ethene) made?**

5. **What is a thermosoftening polymer?**

6. **What happens when a thermosetting polymer is heated for the first time?**

7. **How can we change the properties of polymers?**

8. **Give two examples where polymers have been designed for specific uses.**

---

students' book
page 184 C1b 4.1 **Cracking hydrocarbons**

KEY POINTS

1 Cracking of fractions from crude oil produces smaller, more useful molecules.
2 Alkanes and unsaturated hydrocarbons called alkenes are produced.
3 We can use bromine water to test for unsaturation.

Ethene

double bond

Ethene has a carbon–carbon double bond in it

Fractions from crude oil can be broken down by thermal decomposition in a catalytic cracker. The fraction is vaporised and passed over a hot catalyst, which causes the molecules to split apart and form smaller molecules.

Some of the smaller molecules are alkanes, but some are alkenes that contain carbon–carbon double bonds.

- Alkenes are unsaturated, because they contain fewer hydrogen atoms than alkanes with the same number of carbon atoms.
- Their general formula is C_nH_{2n}.
- They are hydrocarbons, like alkanes, and so burn in air.
- However, they are more reactive than alkanes. So alkenes will react with bromine water turning the orange-yellow solution colourless.

Key words: catalytic cracker, alkenes, C_nH_{2n}, bromine water

GET IT RIGHT!

'Unsaturated' means that the molecule contains fewer hydrogen atoms than an alkane molecule with the same number of carbon atoms.

AQA EXAMINER SAYS...

Make sure you use the correct words to describe the results of the bromine water test – it turns colourless (colour removed) *not* clear (which just means that you can see through it).

CHECK YOURSELF

1 What type of reaction is cracking?

2 What causes the molecules to split apart?

3 What are alkenes?

4 How can you test for unsaturation?

Making polymers from alkenes

Polymers are very large molecules made from many small molecules that have joined together. The small molecules used to make polymers are called monomers.

Lots of ethene molecules can join together in long chains to form poly(ethene), commonly called polythene. The reaction is called addition polymerisation, because the molecules simply add together and only the polymer is produced.

We can react other alkenes together in a similar way to form polymers such as poly(propene). Many of the plastics we use as bags, bottles, containers and toys are made from alkenes.

Key words: monomers, polymers, addition polymerisation, poly(ethene), poly(propene)

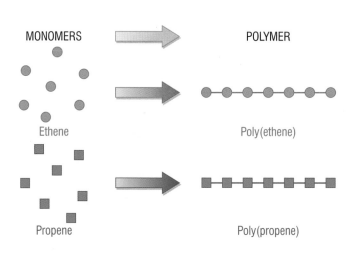

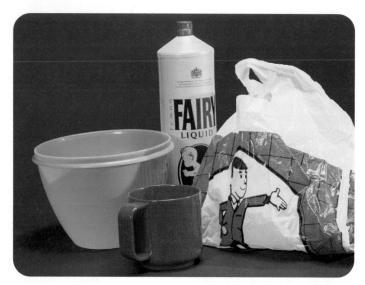

Polymers produced from oil are all around us and are part of our everyday lives

CHECK YOURSELF

1 What are monomers?
2 What is the chemical name of the polymer formed from ethene?
3 Why are polymers formed from alkenes called 'addition polymers'?
4 How are polymers made from alkenes used?

AQA EXAMINER SAYS...

Many students in their answers do not make it clear whether they are describing chemical bonds or intermolecular forces. Chemical bonds are strong and join atoms together to make molecules. Intermolecular forces act between molecules and are weaker than chemical bonds. It is best to use the word 'bond' only for forces that hold atoms together within molecules.

GET IT RIGHT!

Thermosoftening plastics become soft when heated.

Plastic kettles are made out of thermosetting plastics

Polymers have very long molecules that form a tangled mass, rather like spaghetti. This gives them strength with flexibility.

The strands of spaghetti are like the polymer molecules in a plastic

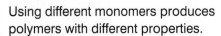

Using different monomers produces polymers with different properties.

● Thermosoftening polymers have weak intermolecular forces between their molecules, so when they are heated they become soft. Then when they cool down, they harden again. This means they can be heated to mould them into shape and they can also be remoulded by heating them again.
● When thermosetting polymers are heated for the first time, chemical bonds form between the polymer molecules. They link together in a giant network. These strong bonds make the plastic set hard and it cannot be softened again by heating.

The forces between the molecules in poly(ethene) are relatively weak. This means that this plastic softens fairly easily when heated.

We use thermosoftening plastics where flexibility is important and where they are not exposed to very high temperatures. Thermosetting plastics are more rigid and can withstand higher temperatures.

Key words: thermosoftening, thermosetting

CHECK YOURSELF

1 Why are polymers strong and flexible?
2 Why can a thermosoftening plastic be remoulded?
3 Why do thermosetting plastics set hard when heated?
4 What type of plastic would be best to make a garden hosepipe?

C1b 4.4 New and useful polymers

EXAMINER SAYS...

You do not need to remember the names and technical details of specific polymers. However, make sure you can recognise the types of polymer from a description of their properties or uses.

EXAM HINTS

You should be able to explain why polymers have replaced other materials.

We can design the properties of polymers by choosing different monomers and by changing the conditions used to make them.

Polymers are widely used for food packaging to keep food in good condition. Some of these polymers are not biodegradable and cause problems with waste disposal.

The polymers used for drinks bottles are strong, flexible, lightweight, clear and non-porous.

Polymers have been developed to coat fabrics that make them waterproof but able to let gases through (breathable). New polymers have been developed for medical use, including hydrogels which are also used in agriculture and food. Smart polymers can be used to control the release of drugs and shape memory polymers are used for stitching wounds.

Key words: hydrogels, smart polymers, shape memory polymers

CHECK YOURSELF

1 How can we make polymers with different properties?

2 Why are polymers widely used in food packaging?

3 How do new polymers help people keep comfortable when they are outdoors in wet weather?

4 Give one example of a new type of polymer designed for medical use.

When a shape memory polymer is used to stitch a wound loosely, the temperature of the body makes the thread tighten and close the wound, applying just the right amount of force. Later, after the wound is healed, the material is designed to dissolve and is harmlessly absorbed by the body.

C1b 4 End of chapter questions

1 Why are fractions from crude oil cracked?

2 How are alkenes different from alkanes with the same number of carbon atoms?

3 Why is the reaction used to make poly(ethene) called addition polymerisation?

4 Name an alkene that can be used to make a polymer other than poly(ethene).

5 What type of force is between the polymer chains in a thermosoftening plastic?

6 Why is it not possible to remould a thermosetting plastic?

7 Suggest two reasons why drinks bottles are often made of plastic rather than glass.

8 What type of new polymers have many uses in medicine, agriculture and food?

1. What are the two main uses of vegetable oils?

2. How are vegetable oils extracted?

3. Why is fast food often cooked in oil?

4. What has been done to a hydrogenated oil?

5. What is an emulsion?

6. Why are emulsifiers added to some foods?

7. What is a food additive?

8. What are the E numbers on food labels?

9. What is biodiesel?

10. Why is biodiesel a good alternative to fossil fuels?

---

students' book page 196   C1b 5.1   **Extracting vegetable oils**

KEY POINTS

1. Vegetable oils can be extracted from seeds, nuts and fruits by pressing or by distillation.
2. Vegetable oils provide a lot of energy as foods or fuels.
3. Some vegetable oils are unsaturated because their molecules contain carbon–carbon double bonds.

Some seeds, nuts and fruits are rich in vegetable oils. The oils can be extracted by pressing followed by removing water and other impurities. Some oils are extracted by distilling the plants mixed with water. This produces a mixture of oil and water from which the oil can be separated.

The molecules in vegetable oils have hydrocarbon chains. Those with carbon–carbon double bonds are unsaturated. If there are several double bonds in each molecule, they are called polyunsaturated. Unsaturated oils will react with bromine or iodine. Bromine water is used as the test for an unsaturated compound.

Vegetable oils produce a lot of energy when eaten or when we burn them as fuels.

Key words: pressing, distilling, unsaturated, decolourise

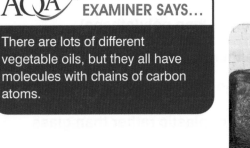

AQA EXAMINER SAYS...

There are lots of different vegetable oils, but they all have molecules with chains of carbon atoms.

Crushing olives before extracting the oil

CHECK YOURSELF

1. What two methods are used to extract vegetable oils?

2. Why are vegetable oils important as foods *and* fuels?

3. What is meant by an unsaturated oil?

4. What can you use to test an oil for unsaturation?

C1b 5.2 Cooking with vegetable oils

EXAMINER SAYS...

Increasing the temperature makes chemical reactions go faster, so food cooks faster in oil than in water.

GET IT RIGHT!

Oils are liquid at room temperature, fats are solid.

The boiling points of vegetable oils are higher than water, so food is cooked at higher temperatures in oil. This means it cooks faster. It also changes the flavour, colour and texture of the food. Some of the oil is absorbed and so the energy content of the food increases.

Unsaturated oils can be reacted with hydrogen so that some or all of the double carbon–carbon bonds become single bonds. This is an addition reaction called hydrogenation and is done at about 60°C using a nickel catalyst. Hydrogenation is used to increase the melting points of oils so they harden and become solid fats at room temperature.

Solid fats can be spread and can be used to make cakes, biscuits and pastries.

Key word: hydrogenation

CHECK YOURSELF

1 Why does food cook faster in hot oil than in boiling water?
2 In what four ways is food cooked in oil different from food cooked in water?
3 What type of chemical reaction is hydrogenation?
4 Why are oils hydrogenated?

C1b 5.3 Everyday emulsions

Emulsions are made from liquids that usually separate from each other. They are made by vigorously shaking, stirring or beating the liquids together to form tiny droplets of the liquids. The droplets are so small that they remain suspended in each other and are slow to separate.

Emulsifiers help keep the droplets to stay suspended and stop the liquids from separating. They do this because different parts of their molecules are attracted to the different liquids.

Emulsions are opaque and usually thicker than the liquids they are made from. This improves their texture, appearance and ability to stick to solids.

Milk, sauces, salad dressings and ice cream are examples of emulsions.

Key words: emulsifiers

EXAMINER SAYS...

Emulsions are different from solutions. In a solution the substances mix completely and the liquid becomes clear. In an emulsion the liquids remain as tiny droplets and the mixture is not transparent.

GET IT RIGHT!

Liquids that do not mix and usually separate from each other can be made into emulsions.

CHECK YOURSELF

1 How are emulsions made?
2 How do emulsifiers work?
3 How is an emulsion different from the liquids it is made from?

What is added to our food?

Substances added to foods to improve its appearance, flavour, texture and keeping qualities are called additives. Additives may be natural products or synthetic chemicals.

Some substances, like salt, vinegar and sugar have been used for hundreds of years.

There are six main types of additive:

- colours
- preservatives
- antioxidants
- emulsifiers
- acidity regulators
- flavourings.

In the European Union only permitted substances may be added to food and these are given E-numbers. Additives must be included in the list of ingredients on food labels, and can be labelled with their full name or their E-number.

Foods are checked by chemical analysis to ensure only permitted additives have been used. The methods used include chromatography and mass spectrometry.

Key words: additives, E-numbers, chromatography, mass spectrometry

AQA↗ EXAMINER SAYS...

Questions are likely to be about the reasons for adding substances to food and how these are detected. You do not have to remember specific E-numbers, but should recognise that a substance is a permitted additive if it has an E-number.

EXAM HINTS

Familiarise yourself with lists of ingredients on the labels of foods you eat so you can recognise additives.

BUMP UP YOUR GRADE

For higher grades you should be able to present arguments for and against the use of additives in foods.

AND TOMATO FLAVOUR SAUCE *AND A SACHET OF TOMATO SAUCE*

Ingredients: Wheatflour, Vegetable Oil with Antioxidants (E320, E321), Cheese & Tomato Flavour [Flavour Enhancer (621), Flavouring, Colours (E102, E110, E124, 154), Acidity Regulators (E262, E331), Acetic Acid, Citric Acid, Artificial Sweetener (Saccharin)], Maltodextrin, Salt, Tomato, Sweetcorn, Chives, Preservative (E220), Sachet: Tomato Sauce.

CHECK YOURSELF

1 What are the four main reasons for adding substances to food?

2 Why are some substances given E-numbers?

3 How could you tell from a label that a food has additives?

4 What can be done to check if substances have been added to a food?

C1b 5.5 Vegetable oils as fuels

KEY POINTS

1 We can burn vegetable oils to produce energy.
2 Modified vegetable oils can replace some of the fossil fuels we use.
3 Biodiesel is renewable and causes less pollution than fossil fuels.

Vegetable oils produce a lot of energy when they burn. They can be treated to remove some chemicals and then used as fuel in diesel engines. We can use waste vegetable oils from food frying as well as fresh oils.

Biodiesel can replace some or all of the diesel fuel produced from crude oil. Biodiesel is renewable because plants are grown to produce the vegetable oils. The plant material left after removing the oil can be used as food for animals.

Biodiesel is less harmful to the environment than fossil fuels. The plants remove carbon dioxide from the air as they grow and so when we burn it there is no additional carbon dioxide released. Biodiesel produces no sulfur dioxide and it is more biodegradable than diesel oil.

Key words: biodiesel, biodegradable, renewable

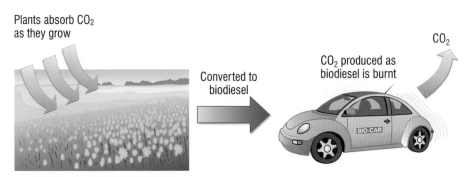

Plants absorb CO_2 as they grow

Converted to biodiesel

CO_2 produced as biodiesel is burnt

CO_2

Cars run on biodiesel produce very little CO_2 overall, as CO_2 is absorbed by the plants which are the raw material for the fuel

CHECK YOURSELF

1 Why is biodiesel renewable?

2 How does biodiesel help with disposal of food waste?

3 Why is biodiesel less harmful to the environment than fossil fuels?

C1b 5 End of chapter questions

1 Describe the method to extract vegetable oils without using heat.

2 How could you test an oil for unsaturation?

3 Why does the energy content of food cooked in oil increase?

4 What is done to harden vegetable oils?

5 What sort of substances are used to make an emulsion?

6 Give two examples of foods that are emulsions.

7 What type of additive helps food stay fresh for longer?

8 What method can be used to check for artificial colours in foods?

9 Why does biodiesel not put additional carbon dioxide into the atmosphere?

10 Why are spillages of biodiesel less harmful to animals than diesel from crude oil?

1. What are the main layers of the Earth?

2. How thick is the Earth's crust?

3. Which parts of the Earth make up tectonic plates?

4. Where was new evidence for tectonic plates found in the 1960s?

5. What was the main gas in the Earth's early atmosphere?

6. How was oxygen in the atmosphere produced?

7. What is the main gas in the Earth's atmosphere now?

8. Which unreactive gases make up about 1% of the atmosphere?

9. What processes release carbon dioxide into the atmosphere?

10. What processes remove carbon dioxide from the atmosphere?

---

students' book page 210

C1b 6.1 — Structure of the Earth

KEY POINTS

1 The Earth is made up of layers – the crust, the mantle and the core.

2 Scientists thought that mountains and valleys formed by the Earth shrinking.

- The Earth is almost spherical with a radius of about 6400 km. At the surface is a thin, solid crust. The thickness of the crust varies between 5 km and 70 km. It is thinnest under the oceans.
- The mantle is under the crust. It is about 3000 km thick, and so goes almost halfway to the centre of the Earth. The mantle is almost entirely solid, but it can flow very slowly.
- The core is very dense and made of metals, mainly nickel and iron. The outer core is liquid and the inner core is solid. This model of the Earth was built up using evidence from seismic waves from earthquakes.

Scientists once thought that mountains and valleys were formed by the Earth shrinking. They believed that the crust solidified as the Earth cooled down and then the Earth continued to shrink, causing the crust to wrinkle.

Key words: crust, mantle, core

GET IT RIGHT!

The inner core is solid and the outer core is liquid.

CHECK YOURSELF

1 Draw a circle with a radius of 6.4 cm to represent the Earth. Draw another circle to show the mantle and core. Calculate how thick the crust should be on your drawing.

2 What is the difference between the outer core and the inner core?

3 Explain how scientists thought that shrinking caused mountains.

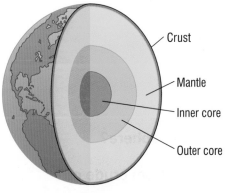

Crust

Mantle

Inner core

Outer core

The structure of the Earth

C1b 6.2 The restless Earth

KEY POINTS

1 The Earth's lithosphere is cracked into pieces called 'tectonic plates'.
2 Convection currents in the mantle cause the tectonic plates to move.
3 Mountains form and earthquakes and volcanoes occur at plate boundaries.
4 Wegener's theory of continental drift was not accepted for many years.

Scientists now believe that mountains form at boundaries between tectonic plates. Tectonic plates are large parts of the lithosphere, the Earth's crust and upper part of the mantle. The lithosphere is broken into tectonic plates that move a few centimetres a year.

Natural radioactivity in the Earth produces heat. This causes convection currents in the mantle that move the plates. At the plate boundaries, huge forces push up the crust to form mountains and cause earthquakes and volcanoes.

Key words: tectonic plates, lithosphere, convection currents, plate boundaries

AQA EXAMINER SAYS...

Alfred Wegener proposed the idea of continental drift in 1915. Other scientists did not accept his ideas. Eventually, in the 1960s, scientists found new evidence deep down on the ocean floor and Wegener's ideas were used to develop the theory of plate tectonics.

The distribution of volcanoes around the world largely follows the boundaries of the tectonic plates

CHECK YOURSELF

1 What are tectonic plates?
2 Explain why tectonic plates move.
3 What three things are likely to happen at plate boundaries?
4 Why were Wegener's ideas not accepted for many years?

C1b 6.3 The Earth's atmosphere in the past

KEY POINTS

1 Volcanoes released most of the gases that formed the Earth's early atmosphere.
2 The gases were mainly carbon dioxide, with some water vapour.
3 The water vapour condensed to form the oceans as the Earth cooled down.
4 Plants evolved and produced oxygen, taking in carbon dioxide.

Scientists think the Earth was formed about 4.5 billion years ago. In the first billion years the surface was covered with volcanoes that released carbon dioxide, water vapour and nitrogen.

As the Earth cooled, most of the water vapour condensed to form the oceans. So the early atmosphere was mainly carbon dioxide with some nitrogen and water vapour. There may have been small amounts of methane and ammonia as well.

In the next two billion years, algae and plants evolved. They used carbon dioxide for photosynthesis to produce food and this released oxygen. As the number of plants increased, the amount of carbon dioxide in the atmosphere decreased and the amount of oxygen increased.

Key words: volcanoes, algae, plants, photosynthesis

AQA EXAMINER SAYS...

There are alternative theories about the Earth's formation and early atmosphere, but many scientists think this one is the most likely.

GET IT RIGHT!

There was very little or no oxygen in the Earth's early atmosphere.

CHECK YOURSELF

1 What produced much of the carbon dioxide, nitrogen and water vapour in the early atmosphere?
2 What happened to most of the water vapour?
3 What process produced oxygen in the atmosphere?

C1b 6.4 Gases in the atmosphere

KEY POINTS

1 The main gases in the atmosphere are nitrogen (78%) and oxygen (21%).
2 There are small amounts of other gases, including carbon dioxide (0.04%), noble gases (almost 1%) and water vapour.

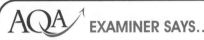

EXAMINER SAYS...

Many students confuse the percentages of oxygen and nitrogen, thinking that there is more oxygen than nitrogen in the air. Also, some think there is much more carbon dioxide than 0.04%.

GET IT RIGHT!

Noble means unreactive.

For the last 200 million years the proportions of the gases in the atmosphere have been about the same as they are now. The atmosphere is almost four-fifths nitrogen and just over one-fifth oxygen.

The other gases make up about 1% of the atmosphere. They are the noble gases (mainly argon), carbon dioxide (0.04%) and water vapour.

Most of the carbon dioxide in the early atmosphere ended up in sedimentary rocks or fossil fuels.

The noble gases are in Group 0 of the periodic table. They are the least reactive elements and they are used where a lack of reactivity is important.

- **Argon** is used as an inert atmosphere, for example in light bulbs to prevent the filament from burning.
- **Neon** is used in electrical discharge tubes for advertising.
- **Helium** is used in balloons.

Key words: noble gases, argon, neon, helium

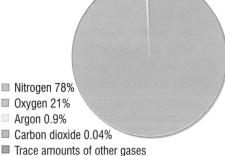

- Nitrogen 78%
- Oxygen 21%
- Argon 0.9%
- Carbon dioxide 0.04%
- Trace amounts of other gases

The relative proportions of nitrogen, oxygen and other gases in the Earth's atmosphere

CHECK YOURSELF

1 For how long has the atmosphere been about the same as it is now?
2 What is the third most abundant gas in dry air?
3 Where did most of the carbon dioxide from the early atmosphere end up?
4 Why are the noble gases so useful?

C1b 6.5 The carbon cycle

KEY POINTS

1 The carbon cycle maintains the level of carbon dioxide in the atmosphere.
2 Carbon moves into the atmosphere by respiration, decomposition and combustion.
3 Carbon is removed from the atmosphere by photosynthesis, and by dissolving in water (mainly the oceans).

GET IT RIGHT!

We are releasing the carbon from fossil fuels very quickly compared with the millions of years taken for them to form.

Carbon dioxide moves into and out of the atmosphere and natural processes have kept this in balance for millions of years.

- Plants remove carbon dioxide from the air for photosynthesis to produce food.
- Carbon dioxide is released back into the atmosphere when plants and animals respire or decompose.
- Some of the carbon is used to make animal shells, and in the past these formed sedimentary rocks.
- Volcanoes produce carbon dioxide by decomposing carbonate rocks that have moved deep into the ground.
- Carbon in plants and animals also went into fossil fuels.
- When we burn fossil fuels we release carbon dioxide that had been absorbed from the atmosphere millions of years ago. Combustion of fossil fuels has increased very rapidly in the last 50 years and the level of carbon dioxide in the atmosphere is increasing.
- As the amount of carbon dioxide increases more of it dissolves in the oceans.

Key words: photosynthesis, respire, decompose, combustion, dissolves

The carbon cycle has kept the level of carbon dioxide in the atmosphere steady for the last 200 million years

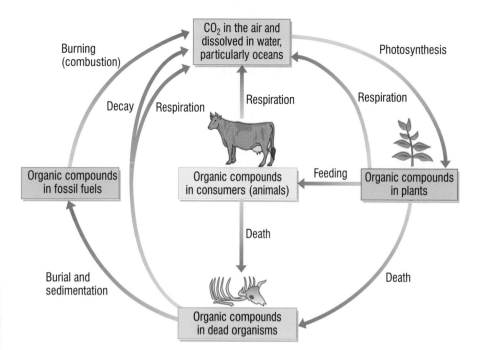

EXAM HINTS

Make sure you know the meanings of the key words.

CHECK YOURSELF

1 What happens to most of the carbon dioxide absorbed by plants?

2 What is the main way, other than through plants, that carbon dioxide is removed from the atmosphere?

3 What is the main reason for the recent increase of the amount of carbon dioxide in the atmosphere?

C1b 6   End of chapter questions

1 The average thickness of the Earth's crust is 32 km. What percentage of the Earth's radius is crust?

2 What are the main features of the Earth's mantle?

3 Why do mountains form at tectonic plate boundaries?

4 What caused Wegener's ideas to be accepted in the 1960s?

5 Name three gases that scientists think were in the early atmosphere.

6 Why did the amount of carbon dioxide decrease as plants increased?

7 Nitrogen and oxygen make up most of the atmosphere now. What other gases are in the atmosphere?

8 Why is helium used in balloons?

9 How do volcanoes produce carbon dioxide?

10 How do the oceans remove carbon dioxide from the atmosphere?

1 Match the types of polymer A, B, C and D with their correct use (i)–(iv).

   A light sensitive   B shape memory
   C thermosetting   D thermosoftening

   (i) bag for frozen food   (ii) saucepan handle
   (iii) sticking plaster   (iv) stitches for a wound

2 Match the names of parts of the Earth A, B, C and D with labels (i)–(iv) on the diagram.

   A core   B crust
   C lithosphere   D mantle

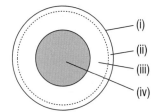

3 Match the names of the foods A, B, C and D with the numbers (i)–(iv) in the table.

   A butter   B cream
   C hydrogenated vegetable oil   D olive oil

Number	Description
(i)	an emulsion of fat in water
(ii)	an emulsion of water in fat
(iii)	produced by cold pressing
(iv)	produced by hardening

4 This question is about the vegetable oils in the table.

Match the oils A, B, C and D with the descriptions (i)–(iv).

   (i) This oil has the highest iodine value because it has the most double bonds.

   (ii) This oil is high in polyunsaturated fats but has the lowest yield.

   (iii) This oil is stable when used for cooking and is high in mono-unsaturated fats.

   (iv) This oil has a low iodine value that makes it suitable for use in diesel engines but cannot be used in cool climates.

5 This question is about waste plastic and glass.

Match the words A, B, C and D with the spaces (i)–(iv) in the sentences.

   A compared   B mixed
   C recycled   D separated

Thermoplastics can be remoulded when they are heated, but most thermoplastic waste is dumped into landfill sites, unlike glass, much of which is (i) . . . . There are several reasons why it is more difficult and less cost effective to recycle thermoplastics. Glass can be easily (ii) . . . into three main types by colour, but it is more difficult to sort thermoplastics because they appear to be very similar. Food containers are often made from (iii) . . . plastics that are very difficult to separate. Thermoplastics are lightweight and the average household uses only a small mass of plastic (iv) . . . with glass.

6 This question is about cracking fractions from crude oil.

   (i) Catalytic cracking is an example of:
      A fractional distillation
      B precipitation
      C thermal decomposition
      D unsaturation

   (ii) Cracking is done to produce more:
      A high boiling fuels and alkanes
      B high boiling fuels and alkenes
      C low boiling fuels and alkanes
      D low boiling fuels and alkenes

   (iii) Which formula completes the equation to show the cracking of decane?

$$C_{10}H_{22} \rightarrow C_5H_{12} + C_2H_4 + \ldots$$

      A C_2H_4 B C_3H_6
      C C_4H_8 D C_5H_{10}

   (iv) When bromine water is shaken with an alkene it:
      A goes cloudy
      B remains orange-yellow
      C turns colourless
      D turns green

	Name of oil	Yield (kg oil per hectare)	Melting point (°C)	Saturated fats (%)	Mono-unsaturated fats (%)	Polyunsaturated fats (%)
A	coconut	2260	25	85	6	2
B	corn	145	−15	14	30	51
C	olive	1019	−6	10	85	0
D	sunflower	800	−17	8	25	67

7 Some students made a solution of the colours from a red sweet. They drew a pencil line near the bottom of a piece of chromatography paper. They put a spot of the solution onto the pencil line. They added spots of three common permitted red colours, E123, E124, 4R and E127. The paper was developed and the results are shown in the diagram.

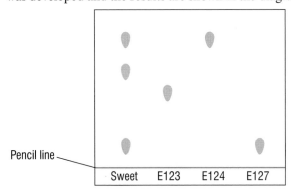

Pencil line

Sweet   E123   E124   E127

(i)   Which permitted colours were in the sweet?
   A   E123 and E124   B   E123 and E127
   C   E124 and E127   D   E123, E124 and E127

(ii) What is the best conclusion?
   The sweet contains . . .
   A   three permitted colours
   B   three artificial colours
   C   three colours, two of which are permitted
   D   three colours, all of which are permitted

(iii) How was the chromatogram developed?
   The paper was . . .
   A   placed in a tray and covered with solvent for a few minutes
   B   placed with the bottom edge in solvent until the solvent reached the top of the paper
   C   sprayed with a solution of a chemical that reacted with the spots
   D   placed in an oven and heated to 100°C for 10 minutes

(iv) Why are only some colours permitted in food?
   Some colours . . .
   A   are expensive   B   are too bright
   C   are toxic   D   break down easily

8 Some fractions from crude oil are converted into more useful substances.

Fraction from crude oil $\xrightarrow[\text{over a hot catalyst}]{\text{vaporised and passed}}$ alkanes + alkenes

(i)   What happens to the molecules in the crude oil fraction when they are passed over the hot catalyst?
   A   addition polymerisation
   B   condensation
   C   distillation
   D   thermal decomposition

(ii) Why are the alkanes that are produced more useful as fuels than the fraction from crude oil?
   A   They are unsaturated.
   B   They do not ignite as easily.
   C   They have higher boiling points.
   D   They have smaller molecules.

(iii) Alkenes can be used to make polymers because they react by:
   A   addition   B   division
   C   multiplication   D   subtraction

(iv) The polymers made from alkenes are:
   A   biodegradable   B   light sensitive
   C   thermosetting   D   thermosoftening

9 The diagram represents the carbon cycle. The figures show the mass of carbon in Gt (gigatonnes) moving between the parts of the cycle each year.
[1 Gt = 1000 million tonnes]

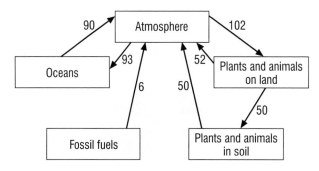

(i)   By how much is the amount of carbon in the atmosphere increasing each year?
   A   2 Gt   B   3 Gt
   C   6 Gt   D   53 Gt

(ii) Which process removes most carbon from the atmosphere?
   A   decomposition of plant and animal remains
   B   dissolving in the oceans
   C   photosynthesis by plants
   D   respiration by plants and animals

(iii) Which of these is only releasing carbon into the atmosphere?
   A   fossil fuels
   B   oceans
   C   plants and animals in soil
   D   plants and animals on land

(iv) In which of these is the amount of carbon increasing?
   A   fossil fuels
   B   oceans
   C   plants and animals in soil
   D   plants and animals on land

P1a | Energy and energy resources

Checklist

This spider diagram shows the topics in the unit. You can copy it out and add your notes and questions around it, or cross off each section when you feel confident you know it for your exams.

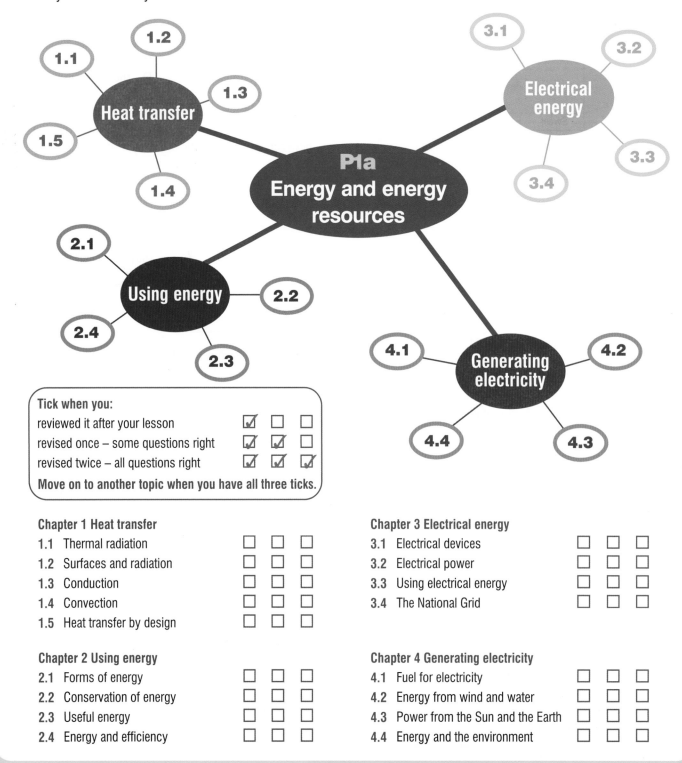

Tick when you:

reviewed it after your lesson	☑	☐	☐
revised once – some questions right	☑	☑	☐
revised twice – all questions right	☑	☑	☑

Move on to another topic when you have all three ticks.

Chapter 1 Heat transfer

1.1	Thermal radiation	☐	☐	☐
1.2	Surfaces and radiation	☐	☐	☐
1.3	Conduction	☐	☐	☐
1.4	Convection	☐	☐	☐
1.5	Heat transfer by design	☐	☐	☐

Chapter 2 Using energy

2.1	Forms of energy	☐	☐	☐
2.2	Conservation of energy	☐	☐	☐
2.3	Useful energy	☐	☐	☐
2.4	Energy and efficiency	☐	☐	☐

Chapter 3 Electrical energy

3.1	Electrical devices	☐	☐	☐
3.2	Electrical power	☐	☐	☐
3.3	Using electrical energy	☐	☐	☐
3.4	The National Grid	☐	☐	☐

Chapter 4 Generating electricity

4.1	Fuel for electricity	☐	☐	☐
4.2	Energy from wind and water	☐	☐	☐
4.3	Power from the Sun and the Earth	☐	☐	☐
4.4	Energy and the environment	☐	☐	☐

What are you expected to know?

Chapter 1 Heat transfer (See students' book pages 228–239)

- Heat energy is transferred by conduction, convection and radiation.
- Conduction and convection involve particles but radiation does not.
- Dark, matt surfaces are good absorbers and good emitters of heat radiation.
- Light, shiny surfaces are poor absorbers and poor emitters of heat radiation.
- The rate at which something radiates heat depends on its surface area and how much hotter it is than its surroundings.

Chapter 2 Using energy (See students' book pages 242–251)

- Energy cannot be created or destroyed, just transformed from one form to another.
- Not all energy transformations are useful, some energy is always 'wasted'.
- All energy is eventually transferred to the surroundings, which become warmer.
- Efficiency $= \dfrac{\text{useful energy transferred}}{\text{total energy supplied}}$

On a roller coaster – having fun with energy transformations!

Chapter 3 Electrical energy (See students' book pages 254–263)

- Power is the amount of energy transferred each second.
- Power is measured in watts. Their symbol is W.
- Energy is measured in joules. Their symbol is J.
- Electricity is transferred around the country through the National Grid.
- Energy transferred = power x time
- The kilowatt-hour is another unit of energy, which is used to measure the amount of electricity used at home.

An electricity meter

Chapter 4 Generating electricity (See students' book pages 266–275)

- Some power stations use non-renewable sources of energy such as coal and natural gas.
- In nuclear power stations, energy is produced by nuclear fission.
- Renewable energy sources include:
  - wind
  - waves
  - tides
  - falling water
  - the Sun
  - heat from the ground (geothermal energy).
- There are advantages and disadvantages to using both renewable and non-renewable energy sources.

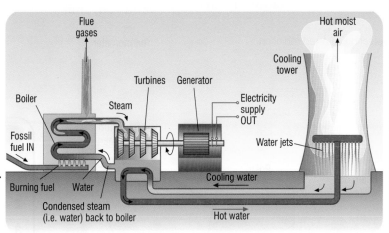

Inside a fossil fuel power station

Pre Test: Heat transfer

1. Which type of heat transfer can occur through a vacuum?

2. Which type of heat transfer does not involve particles?

3. Why are houses in hot countries often painted white?

4. Which teapot will keep tea hot the longest, a light, shiny one or a dull, dark one?

5. Why are metals the best conductors of heat?

6. What is an insulator?

7. Which type of heat transfer sets up currents in fluids?

8. What is convection?

9. What type of heat loss is reduced by cavity wall insulation?

10. What type of heat loss is reduced by carpets?

---

students' book page 228

P1a 1.1 Thermal radiation

KEY POINTS

1. Thermal radiation is energy transfer by electromagnetic waves.
2. All objects emit thermal radiation.
3. The hotter an object is, the more thermal radiation it emits.

Thermal or heat radiation is the transfer of energy by infra-red waves. These waves are part of the electromagnetic spectrum.

- All objects emit (give off) heat radiation.
- The hotter the object the more heat radiation it emits.
- Heat radiation can travel through a vacuum like space. This is how we get heat from the Sun.

Key words: thermal, heat, radiation, infra-red, emit

GET IT RIGHT!

Transfer of heat energy by infra-red radiation does **not** involve particles.

Detecting infra-red radiation

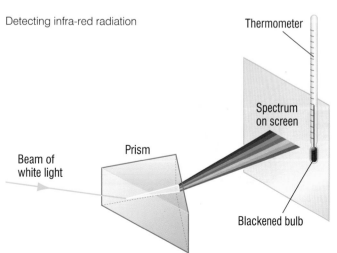

Thermometer

Spectrum on screen

Prism

Beam of white light

Blackened bulb

CHECK YOURSELF

1. Which part of the electromagnetic spectrum is concerned with heat energy?

2. How does heat from the Sun reach the Earth?

3. Do all objects give out the same amount of heat radiation? Explain your answer.

P1a 1.2 Surfaces and radiation

KEY POINTS

1 Dark, matt surfaces are better emitters of thermal radiation than light, shiny surfaces.
2 Dark, matt surfaces are better absorbers of thermal radiation than light, shiny surfaces.

- Dark, matt surfaces are good absorbers of radiation. An object painted dull black and left in the Sun will become hotter than the same object painted shiny white.
- Dark, matt surfaces are also good emitters of radiation. So an object that is painted dull black will lose heat and cool down quicker that the same object painted shiny white.

Key words: absorber, emitter

AQA EXAMINER SAYS...

Exam questions often involve different applications of absorption and emission.

GET IT RIGHT!

Don't be fooled by most central heating radiators that are covered in glossy white paint. The best radiators of heat are dark, matt surfaces.

Remember that an object that is warmer than the surroundings will lose heat energy and cool down. On the other hand, an object that is cooler than the surroundings will gain heat energy and warm up.

CHECK YOURSELF

1 Which surfaces are the best emitters of heat radiation?

2 Which surfaces are the best absorbers of heat radiation?

3 Why are the pipes on the back of a fridge usually painted black?

P1a 1.3 Conduction

KEY POINTS

1 Conduction in a metal is due mainly to free electrons transferring energy inside the metal.
2 Non-metals are poor conductors because they do not contain free electrons.
3 Materials such as fibreglass are good insulators because they contain pockets of trapped air.

Conduction occurs mainly in solids. Most liquids and all gases are poor conductors.

- If one end of a solid is heated, the particles at that end gain kinetic energy and vibrate more. This energy is passed to neighbouring particles and in this way the heat is transferred through the solid.

This process occurs in metals.

- In addition, when metals are heated their free electrons gain kinetic energy and move through the metal transferring energy by colliding with other particles. Hence all metals are good conductors of heat.
- Poor conductors are called insulators.

Key words: conduction, conductor, insulator

CHECK YOURSELF

1 Why are materials that trap air, such as fibreglass, good insulators?

2 Why are saucepans often made of metal with wooden handles?

3 Which materials are the best conductors of heat?

AQA EXAMINER SAYS...

Know some examples of insulators and how they are used.

BUMP UP YOUR GRADE

Make sure you can explain why all metals are good conductors of heat energy.

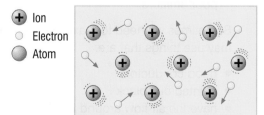

+ Ion
○ Electron
● Atom

Energy transfer in a metal

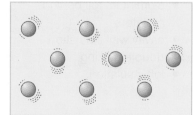

Energy transfer in a non-metal

P1a 1.4 Convection

KEY POINTS

1 Convection takes place only in liquids and gases (fluids).
2 Heating a liquid or a gas makes it less dense.
3 Convection is due to a hot liquid or gas rising.

AQA EXAMINER SAYS...

Remember that convection cannot occur in solids.

The type of surface makes no difference to the amount of conduction or convection from an object – it only affects radiated heat energy.

BUMP UP YOUR GRADE

Make sure that you can explain how convection currents are set up in terms of a fluid's changes in density.

Convection occurs in fluids.

When a fluid is heated it expands. The fluid becomes less dense and rises. The warm fluid is replaced by cooler, denser fluid. The resulting convection current transfers heat throughout the fluid.

Convection currents can be on a very small scale, such as heating water in a beaker, or on a very large scale such as heating the air above land and sea. Convection currents are responsible for onshore and offshore breezes.

Key words: fluid, convection, convection current

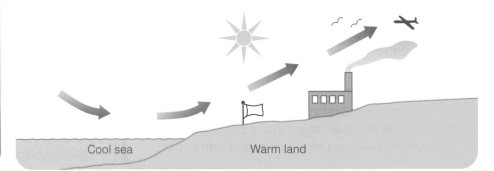

Cool sea   Warm land

CHECK YOURSELF

1 In which states of matter does convection occur?
2 What happens to the density of a fluid when it is heated?
3 Why doesn't convection take place in solids?

P1a 1.5 Heat transfer by design

KEY POINTS

1 A radiator has a large surface area so it can lose heat easily.
2 Small objects lose heat more easily than large objects.
3 Heat loss from a building can be reduced using:
   - aluminium foil behind radiators
   - cavity wall insulation
   - double glazing
   - loft insulation.

In many situations we want to minimise heat loss. We do this by reducing the losses due to conduction, convection and radiation.

- We can reduce heat loss by conduction by using insulators, e.g. trapping a layer of air.
- Heat loss by convection can be reduced by preventing convection currents being set up, e.g. by trapping air in small pockets.
- We can reduce heat loss by radiation by using light, shiny surfaces, which are poor emitters.

Sometimes we need to maximise heat loss to keep things cool. To do this we may use things that are:

- good conductors
- painted dull black
- have the air flow around them maximised.

Key words: maximise, minimise

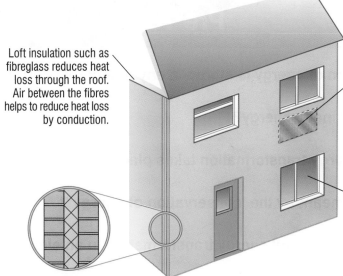

Loft insulation such as fibreglass reduces heat loss through the roof. Air between the fibres helps to reduce heat loss by conduction.

Aluminium foil between a radiator panel and the wall reflects heat radiation away from the wall.

A double glazed window has two glass panes with dry air or a vacuum between the panes. Dry air is a good insulator so it cuts down heat conduction. A vacuum cuts out heat transfer by convection as well.

Cavity wall insulation reduces heat loss through the walls. We place insulation between the two layers of brick that make up the walls of a house.

CHECK YOURSELF

1 What type of heat transfer is reduced by double glazing?

2 How does cavity wall insulation reduce heat loss from a building?

3 What is loft insulation usually made from?

P1a 1   End of chapter questions

1 **Name the three types of heat transfer.**

2 **Which type of heat transfer occurs mainly in solids?**

3 **How are convection currents set up in fluids?**

4 **Describe the process of heat transfer through a metal.**

5 **What factors affect the amount of heat radiated by a body?**

6 **Why are gases poor conductors?**

7 **How does surface colour affect the rate of conduction?**

8 **Why do central heating radiators have large surface areas?**

9 **Why does a concrete floor feel colder to your feet than a carpeted floor at the same temperature?**

10 **Why are hot water tanks often wrapped in glass fibre jackets?**

Pre Test: Using energy

1. What form of energy is stored in any object that can fall?

2. What is kinetic energy?

3. What energy transformation takes place in a microphone?

4. What is meant by the 'conservation of energy'?

5. What is the useful energy transformation in an electric motor?

6. What happens to the energy wasted by a device?

7. What are the units of efficiency?

8. What is the SI unit of energy?

---

students' book page 242

P1a 2.1 Forms of energy

KEY POINTS

1. Energy exists in different forms.
2. Energy can change (transform) from one form into another form.

BUMP UP YOUR GRADE

Make sure you are familiar with the different forms that energy can take and know some examples of each of them.

CHECK YOURSELF

1. What energy do we give to a spring if we squash it?

2. Where does the chemical energy stored in your muscles come from?

3. What form of energy does a moving train have?

Energy exists in different forms such as: light, thermal (heat), sound, kinetic (movement), nuclear, electrical, gravitational potential, elastic potential and chemical.

The last three are forms of stored energy.

Form of energy	Example
Light	From the Sun or a lamp
Thermal (heat)	Flows from a hot object to a colder object
Sound	From a loudspeaker or your voice
Kinetic (movement)	Anything moving
Nuclear	From nuclear reactions
Electrical	Whenever an electric current flows
Gravitational potential	Stored in any object that can fall
Elastic potential (strain)	Stored in stretched objects such as elastic bands or springs
Chemical	Stored in fuels, food and batteries and released when chemical reactions taken place

Energy can transform (change) from one form into another.

Key words: energy, kinetic, potential

P1a 2.2 Conservation of energy

GET IT RIGHT!

Remember that the conservation of energy applies in any situation.

BUMP UP YOUR GRADE

Know some examples of energy transformations.

EXAM HINTS

The conservation of energy is an extremely important idea in physics so it often comes up in examination questions.

It is not possible to create or destroy energy. It is only possible to transform it from one form to another, or transfer (move) it from one place to another.

This means that the total amount of energy is always the same. This is called the **'conservation of energy'**.

For example when an object falls, gravitational potential energy is transformed into kinetic energy. Similarly, stretching an elastic band transforms chemical energy into elastic potential energy. In a solar cell, light energy is transformed into electrical energy.

Key words: transform, transfer, conservation

On a roller coaster – having fun with energy transformations!

CHECK YOURSELF

1 What energy transformation takes place when you burn a fuel?

2 What energy transformations take place in a light bulb?

3 When you run, what type of energy is changed into kinetic energy? Where does this energy come from?

P1a 2.3 Useful energy

KEY POINTS

1 Useful energy is energy in the place we want it and in the form we need it.
2 Wasted energy is energy that is not useful energy.
3 Useful energy and wasted energy both end up being transferred to the surroundings, which become warmer.
4 As energy spreads out, it gets more and more difficult to use for further energy transfers.

AQA EXAMINER SAYS...

Remember that energy cannot be destroyed, so it is better to talk about energy that is 'wasted' than to say that energy is 'lost'.

A device (or machine) is something that transfers energy from one place to another or transforms energy from one form to another.

The energy supplied to the device is called the 'input energy'.

The energy we get out of the device consists of:

● useful energy, which is transferred to the place we want and in the form we want it
● wasted energy which is not usefully transferred or transformed (mostly it is converted as heat, frequently as a result of friction between the moving parts of the device).

From the conservation of energy we know that:

Input energy = useful energy + wasted energy

Both the useful energy and the wasted energy will eventually be transferred to the surroundings, and make them warm up. As it does so, it becomes more difficult to use the energy.

Key words: device, input energy, useful energy, wasted energy

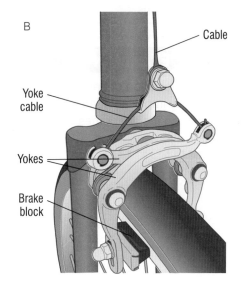

A

B

Cable

Yoke cable

Yokes

Brake block

Friction in action. A) Using a drill, B) braking.

GET IT RIGHT!

In some devices some of the wasted energy may be transferred into sound, but the amount of energy is usually very small. Eventually this energy will end up as heat and make the surroundings warmer.

CHECK YOURSELF

1 What is the useful energy transformation in a light bulb and what happens to the wasted energy?

2 Why does energy become more difficult to use as it spreads out?

3 Why do computers and televisions have vents?

Energy and efficiency

KEY POINTS

1 Energy is measured in joules.
2 The efficiency of a device = useful energy transferred by the device ÷ total energy supplied to the device
3 Wasted energy causes inefficiency.

The unit of energy is the joule, symbol J. This unit is used for all forms of energy.

The less energy that is wasted by a device, the more efficient the device is said to be.

We can calculate the efficiency of a device using the equation in the key points. It can also be written as:

$$\text{Efficiency} = \frac{\text{energy usefully transformed by the device}}{\text{input energy}}$$

The efficiency can be left as a fraction or multiplied by 100 to give a percentage.

No device can be 100% efficient, except an electric heater, which usefully transforms all of the electrical energy supplied to it into heat energy.

Key words: joule, efficiency

AQA EXAMINER SAYS...

Remember that no device (except an electric heater) can be 100% efficient. So if you do an efficiency calculation and the answer is greater than 1 or 100%, you have made an error and should check your working.

GET IT RIGHT!

Efficiency is a ratio. That means it does not have a unit.

EXAM HINTS

Be careful in questions when you substitute energies into the efficiency equation. You may be given the energy usefully transferred, or you may be given the energy wasted and have to subtract this from the input energy to find the energy usefully transferred.

CHECK YOURSELF

1 If a device is adjusted so that it wastes less energy as heat, what happens to its efficiency?

2 In a light bulb, for every 20 joules of energy input to the bulb, 5 joules are usefully transformed into light energy. What is the efficiency of the bulb?

3 In an electric motor 2000 joules of energy are given out as heat to the surroundings for every 5000 joules of electrical energy supplied to the motor. What is the efficiency of the motor?

P1a 2   End of chapter questions

1 **List three forms of stored energy and give an example of each.**

2 **Explain the energy transformations that take place if you climb to the top of a ladder then fall to the ground.**

3 **Why may an electric heater be 100% efficient when no other device ever is?**

4 **Calculate the efficiency of a kettle if it takes 720 000 J of energy to raise the temperature of a kettle full of cold water to boiling point when 750 000 J of energy is supplied to the kettle.**

5 **What happens to the energy that is not used to heat the water?**

6 **What energy do we give to a spring if we stretch it?**

7 **What is the useful energy transformation in a vacuum cleaner?**

8 **What energy transformation takes place in a solar cell?**

Pre Test: Electrical energy

1. What energy transformation takes place in an electric iron?

2. What energy transformations take place in a television?

3. What is meant by the power of a device?

4. What is the unit of power?

5. What unit do electricity companies use to measure the amount of electrical energy used?

6. What is the equation that relates energy, power and time?

7. What is the National Grid?

8. What type of transformer makes voltages larger?

---

students' book
page 254

P1a 3.1 Electrical devices

KEY POINTS

1 Electrical energy is energy transfer due to an electric current.
2 Uses of electrical devices include:
- heating
- lighting
- making objects move (using an electric motor)
- creating sound and visual images.

Electrical devices are extremely useful. They transform electrical energy into whatever form of energy we need at the flick of a switch.

Common electrical devices include:

- kettles, to produce heat energy
- lamps, to produce light
- electric mixers, to produce kinetic energy
- speakers, to produce sound energy
- televisions, to produce light and sound energy.

Key words: electrical devices

Electrical devices

GET IT RIGHT!

Remember that all electrical devices will transform some electrical energy to heat, but this may not be a useful energy transformation.

CHECK YOURSELF

1 What energy transformations take place in an electric drill?

2 How is electrical energy supplied to a torch?

3 What energy transformations take place in a vacuum cleaner?

P1a 3.2 Electrical power

The power of a device is the rate at which it transforms energy.

The unit of power is the watt, symbol W. A device with a power of 1 watt transforms 1 joule of electrical energy to other forms of energy every second.

Often a watt is too small a unit to be useful, so power may be given in kilowatts (kW). 1 kilowatt = 1000 watts.

Power is calculated using the equation:

$$\text{Power (in watts)} = \frac{\text{energy transferred (in joules)}}{\text{time taken (in seconds)}}$$

Key words: power, watt, kilowatt

Muscle power

CHECK YOURSELF

1 How many watts are in 30 kilowatts?

2 Which is more powerful, a 2.5 kW heater or a 3000 W heater?

3 An electric motor transforms 36 kJ of electrical energy into kinetic energy in 3 minutes. What is the useful power output of the motor?

P1a 3.3 Using electrical energy

1 Energy transferred (kW h)
  = power of device (kW) × time (h)
2 Total cost of electricity =
  number of kW h × cost per kW h

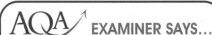

EXAMINER SAYS...

Take care with the units here they are tricky! Remember that the kilowatt-hour is a unit of energy (not power).

Companies that supply mains electricity charge customers for the amount of electrical energy used. The amount of energy is measured in kilowatt-hours, symbol kW h. A kilowatt-hour is the amount of energy that is transferred by a one kilowatt device when used for one hour.

The amount of energy, in kW h, transferred to a mains device can be found by multiplying the power of the device in kilowatts by the time it is used for in hours (see the equation in the key points).

The electricity meter in a house records the number of kW h of energy used. If the previous meter reading is subtracted from the current reading, the electrical energy used between the readings can be calculated. The cost of the electrical energy supplied is found by multiplying the number of kW h by the cost per kW h, which is given on the electricity bill.

Key words: kilowatt-hour, kilowatt, hour

CHECK YOURSELF

1 What quantity is measured in kilowatts?

2 How much electrical energy, in kW h, does it take to use a 9 kW shower for 20 minutes?

3 The price of one kilowatt-hour of electricity is 8 p. How much does it cost to use a 100 W electric light for 4 hours?

An electricity meter

P1a 3.4 The National Grid

1 The National Grid is a network of cables and transformers.
2 We use step-up transformers to step power stations voltages up to the grid voltage.
3 We use step-down transformers to step the grid voltage down for use in our homes.
4 A high grid voltage reduces energy loss and makes the system more efficient.

In Britain, electricity is distributed through the National Grid. This is a network of pylons and cables that connects power stations to homes and other buildings. Since the whole country is connected to the system, power stations can be switched in or out according to demand.

In power stations, electricity is generated at a particular voltage. The voltage is increased by step-up transformers before the electricity is transmitted across the National Grid. This is because transmission at high voltage reduces energy losses in the cables, making the system more efficient.

It would be dangerous to supply electricity to consumers at these very high voltages. So step-down transformers are used to reduce the voltage to 230 volts.

BUMP UP YOUR GRADE

Be able to describe the reasons why voltages are increased and decreased within the National Grid system.

Key words: National Grid, step-up transformer, step-down transformer

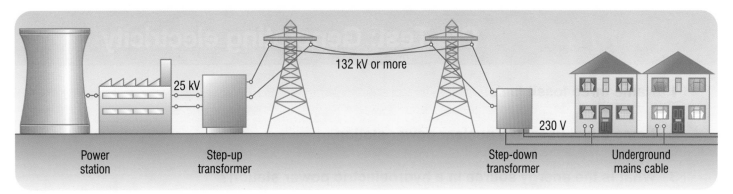

The National Grid

EXAM HINTS

Know the different parts of the National Grid system and the order in which they are used. In an examination question you might have to describe them in words or label them on a diagram.

CHECK YOURSELF

1 What type of transformer makes voltages smaller?

2 Why is electricity transmitted at very high voltages across the National Grid?

3 What type of transformer is found in a local sub-station?

P1a 3   End of chapter questions

1 State an equivalent unit to the watt.

2 What device transforms sound energy to electrical energy?

3 What device transforms electrical energy to sound energy?

4 In a 3 kW kettle how many joules of electrical energy are transformed from electrical energy to heat energy each second?

5 An immersion heater converts 36 000 000 J of electrical energy into heat energy when it is switched on for 1 hour.
What is the power of the heater in kilowatts?

6 How much does it cost to use a 1200 W vacuum cleaner for 10 minutes if electrical energy costs 7 p per kilowatt-hour?

7 Draw a block diagram showing the different parts of the National Grid system and the order in which they are used.

8 Why are voltages reduced to 230 V before reaching homes?

(1) **Name three fossil fuels.**

(2) **Name a fuel used in a nuclear power station.**

(3) **What is the energy source in a hydroelectric power station?**

(4) **What is a wind turbine?**

(5) **What does a solar cell do?**

(6) **What is 'geothermal energy'?**

(7) **Name two renewable energy resources.**

(8) **Suggest an advantage of a nuclear power station.**

---

students' book page 266 **P1a 4.1**   # Fuel for electricity

KEY POINTS

1 Electricity generators in power stations are driven by turbines.
2 Much more energy is released per kilogram from uranium than from fossil fuels.

GET IT RIGHT!

Most power stations burn fuels to produce heat. In a nuclear power station uranium is not burned, the heat comes from a process called nuclear fission.

CHECK YOURSELF

1 Which of the following is *not* a fossil fuel: coal, plutonium, gas, oil?

2 What process produces heat in a nuclear power station?

3 Why is water turned into steam in a coal-fired power station?

In most power stations, water is heated to produce steam. The steam drives a turbine, which is coupled to an electrical generator that produces the electricity.

The heat can come from burning a fuel such as coal, oil or gas (called fossil fuels); or hot gases may drive the turbine directly.

In a nuclear power station, the fuel used is uranium (or sometimes plutonium). The nucleus of a uranium atom can undergo a process called 'fission' that releases energy. There are lots of uranium nuclei, so lots of fission reactions take place, producing lots of heat energy. This energy is used to turn water into steam.

More energy is released from each kilogram of uranium undergoing fission reactions than from each kilogram of fossil fuel that we burn.

Key words: turbine, generator, fossil fuel, fission

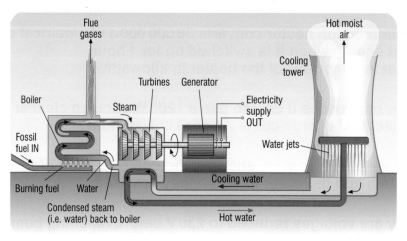

Inside a fossil fuel power station

P1a 4.2 Energy from wind and water

KEY POINTS

1 A wind turbine is an electricity generator on top of a tall tower.
2 A wave generator is a floating generator turned by the waves.
3 Hydroelectricity generators are turned by water running downhill.
4 A tidal power station traps each high tide and uses it to turn generators.

EXAMINER SAYS...

There are a number of different ways that electricity can be generated using energy from water. Exam questions could be asked about any of them so learn them all carefully and make sure you understand the differences between them.

We can use energy from wind and water to drive turbines directly.

- In a wind turbine, the wind passing over the blades makes them rotate and drive a generator at the top of a narrow tower.

Electricity can be produced from energy obtained from falling water, waves or tides.

- At a hydroelectric power station, water which has been collected in a reservoir is allowed to flow downhill and turn turbines at the bottom of the hill.
- In a pumped storage system, surplus electricity is used, at times of low demand, to pump the water back up the hill to the top reservoir.
- This means that the energy is stored, and then at times of high demand the water can be released to fall through the turbines and convert the stored energy to electrical energy.
- We can use the movement of the waves on the sea to generate electricity with devices that float on the water. The movement drives a turbine that turns a generator. Then the electricity is delivered to the grid system on shore by a cable.
- The level of the sea around the coastline rises and falls twice each day. These changes in sea level are called tides. If a barrage is built across a river estuary, the water at each high tide can be trapped behind it. When the water is released to fall down to the lower sea level, it drives turbines.

Key words: wind, waves, hydroelectricity, tides

CHECK YOURSELF

1 Why can't a hydroelectric power station be built in a flat area?

2 What form of energy is stored in the water in the top reservoir of a pumped storage scheme?

3 Why is wave power likely to be less reliable than tidal power?

P1a 4.3 Power from the Sun and the Earth

KEY POINTS

1 We can convert solar energy into electricity using solar cells or use it to heat water directly in solar heating panels.
2 Geothermal energy comes from the energy released by radioactive substances deep inside the Earth.

BUMP UP YOUR GRADE

Adding the details in a description of geothermal energy will earn you extra marks.

Energy from the Sun travels through space to the Earth as electromagnetic radiation. A solar cell can convert this energy into electrical energy. Each cell only produces a small amount of electricity, so they are useful to power small devices such as watches and calculators. We can also join together large numbers of the cells to form a solar panel.

Water flowing through a solar heating panel is heated directly by energy from the Sun.

Heat energy is produced inside the Earth by radioactive processes and this heats the surrounding rock. In a few parts of the world, hot water comes up to the surface naturally and can be used to heat buildings nearby.

In other places, very deep holes are drilled and cold water is pumped down to the hot rocks where it is heated and comes back to the surface as steam. The steam is used to drive turbines that turn generators and so electricity is produced.

Key words: solar energy, geothermal energy

CHECK YOURSELF

1 Where does the geothermal energy that produces heat in the ground come from?

2 What energy transformation takes place in a solar cell?

3 Why are large numbers of solar cells often joined to make a solar panel?

P1a 4.4 Energy and the environment

Coal, oil, gas and uranium are non-renewable energy resources. This means that the rate at which they are used is very much faster than the rate at which they are produced. If we continue to use them up at the current rate they will soon run out.

Renewable energy resources will not run out.

There are advantages and disadvantages to using each type of energy resource:

Energy resource	Advantages	Disadvantages
Coal	• Bigger reserves than the other fossil fuels • Reliable	• Non-renewable • Production of CO_2, a greenhouse gas • Production of SO_2, causing acid rain
Oil	• Reliable	• Non-renewable • Production of CO_2, a greenhouse gas • Production of SO_2, causing acid rain
Gas	• Reliable • Gas power stations can be started up quickly to deal with sudden demand	• Non-renewable • Production of CO_2, a greenhouse gas
Nuclear	• No production of polluting gases • Reliable	• Non-renewable • Produces nuclear waste, which is difficult to dispose of safely • Risk of a big accident, such as Chernobyl
Wind	• Renewable • Free • No production of polluting gases	• Requires many large turbines • Unsightly and noisy • Not reliable, the wind does not always blow
Falling water	• Renewable • Free • No production of polluting gases • Reliable in wet areas • Pumped storage systems allow storage of energy • Can be started up quickly to deal with sudden demand	• Only work in wet and hilly areas • Flooding of an area affects the local ecology
Waves	• Renewable • Free • No production of polluting gases	• Can be a hazard to boats • Not reliable
Tides	• Renewable • Free • No production of polluting gases • Reliable, always tides twice a day	• Only a few river estuaries are suitable • Building a barrage affects the local ecology

Energy resource	Advantages	Disadvantages
Solar	• Renewable • Free • No production of polluting gases • Reliable in hot countries, in the daytime	• Only suitable for small amounts of electricity, or requires large number of cells • Unreliable in less sunny countries
Geothermal	• Renewable • Free • No production of polluting gases	• Only economically viable in a very few places • Drilling through large depth of rock is difficult and expensive

Key words: renewable, non-renewable, polluting

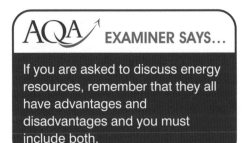

EXAMINER SAYS...

If you are asked to discuss energy resources, remember that they all have advantages and disadvantages and you must include both.

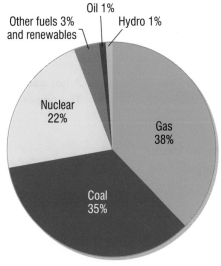

Other fuels 3% and renewables

Oil 1%

Hydro 1%

Nuclear 22%

Gas 38%

Coal 35%

Energy sources for electricity

CHECK YOURSELF

1 Are renewable or non-renewable energy resources the most reliable?

2 Which types of power station can be started up quickly to deal with periods of high demand?

3 What type of area would be most suitable for a wind farm?

P1a 4 — End of chapter questions

1 Explain the difference between renewable and non-renewable energy resources.

2 In which three ways can water be used as an energy resource to generate electricity?

3 How can geothermal energy be used to produce heat and electricity?

4 What are the advantages of using fossil fuels in power stations to produce electricity?

5 What are the disadvantages of using fossil fuels in power stations to produce electricity?

6 Suggest a disadvantage of a nuclear power station.

7 Why is geothermal energy economically unviable in most places?

8 What colour are solar heating panels usually painted?

1 A book is taken out of a bookcase and moved to a higher shelf.

In its new position it has more:

A   elastic potential energy
B   gravitational potential energy
C   kinetic energy
D   thermal energy

2 A motor converts 3000 J of electrical energy to kinetic energy every second. What is the power output of the motor?

A   3 W
B   50 W
C   3 kW
D   3000 kW

3 A filament lamp converts electrical energy to light. For every 100 J of electrical energy supplied to the lamp 10 J is converted to light.

What is the efficiency of the lamp?

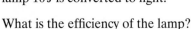

A   0.1
B   1
C   10
D   100

4 Power stations use different energy resources to produce electricity.

Match words A, B, C and D from the list with the numbers (i)–(iv) in the sentences.

A   gas   B   steam
C   uranium   D   water

In many power stations . . . (i) . . . is heated to produce . . . (ii) . . . . This drives a turbine which is coupled to an electrical generator. The heat can come from burning a fuel such as coal, oil or . . . (iii) . . . . In a nuclear power station, the fuel used is . . . (iv) . . . .

5 A vacuum cleaner contains an electric motor.

Match words A, B, C and D from the list with the numbers (i)–(iv) in the sentences.

A   kinetic   B   thermal
C   useful   D   wasted

The motor transforms electrical energy mainly into . . . (i) . . . energy. This is a . . . (ii) . . . energy transformation. Some of the electrical energy is also transformed into . . . (iii) . . . energy and sound energy. This energy is . . . (iv) . . . .

6 A hot water tank contains an electrical heating element. The power rating of the heater is 8 kW.

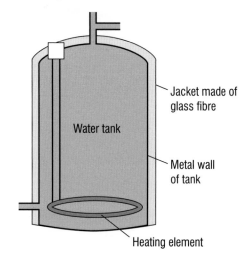

(i)   During one day, the heater is switched on for 4 hours. How much energy will it transfer during this time?
A   2 kWh
B   8 kWh
C   16 kWh
D   32 kWh

(ii) Heat energy spreads through the water by:
A   conduction
B   convection
C   evaporation
D   radiation

(iii) Heat energy is transmitted through the walls of the tank by:
A   conduction
B   convection
C   evaporation
D   radiation

 Test & Assessment Interactive quizzes, answers and hints online!

(iv) The outside of the hot water tank is surrounded by a jacket made from glass fibre. Glass fibre is used because it is a good:

A conductor
B convector
C insulator
D radiator

7 Which of the following would be the best conductor of heat?

A carpet
B coal
C concrete
D copper

8 Which of the following is **not** a method of heat transfer?

A conduction
B convection
C ionisation
D radiation

9 If an object is warmer than the surroundings it will:

A gain heat energy and cool down
B gain heat energy and warm up
C lose heat energy and cool down
D lose heat energy and warm up

10 An electric motor has a power output of 4 kW. How many joules of electrical energy does it convert to kinetic energy each second?

A 4
B 40
C 400
D 4000

11 Electrical energy is transmitted across the country by a system called the National Grid.

Match words A, B, C and D from the list with the numbers (i)–(iv) in the sentences.

A decreased
C power
B increased
D voltage

Electricity is generated in . . . (i) . . . stations at a particular voltage. The . . . (ii) . . . is . . . (iii) . . . by step-up transformers and transmitted across the country. The voltage is . . . (iv) . . . step-down transformers before it reaches consumers.

12 Renewable energy resources can be used to generate electricity.

Match words A, B, C and D from the list with the numbers (i)–(iv) in the sentences.

A waves
C tides
B boats
D estuaries

Power from . . . (i) . . . can be used to generate electricity. It is free but not reliable and the generators can be a hazard to . . . (ii) . . . Power from the . . . (iii) . . . is reliable as they occur twice each day, but only a few . . . (iv) . . . are suitable and building a barrage affects the local ecology.

13 Many different energy resources can be used to generate electricity. There are advantages and disadvantages to both.

(i) Which of these energy resources does **not** produce CO_2 when used to generate electricity?
A coal
B gas
C oil
D uranium

(ii) In a hydroelectric power station the energy resource is falling water. As the water falls the energy transformation that takes place is from:
A gravitational potential energy to kinetic energy
B kinetic energy to electrical energy
C kinetic energy to gravitational potential energy
D thermal energy to kinetic energy

(iii) One disadvantage of hydroelectric power stations is:
A they only work in wet and hilly areas
B they do not produce polluting gases
C they only work when the wind blows
D they do not produce noise pollution

(iv) The process used to produce energy from fuel in a nuclear power station is called:
A burning
B fission
C fusion
D radiation

P1b | Radiation and the Universe

Checklist

This spider diagram shows the topics in the unit. You can copy it out and add your notes and questions around it, or cross off each section when you feel confident you know it for your exams.

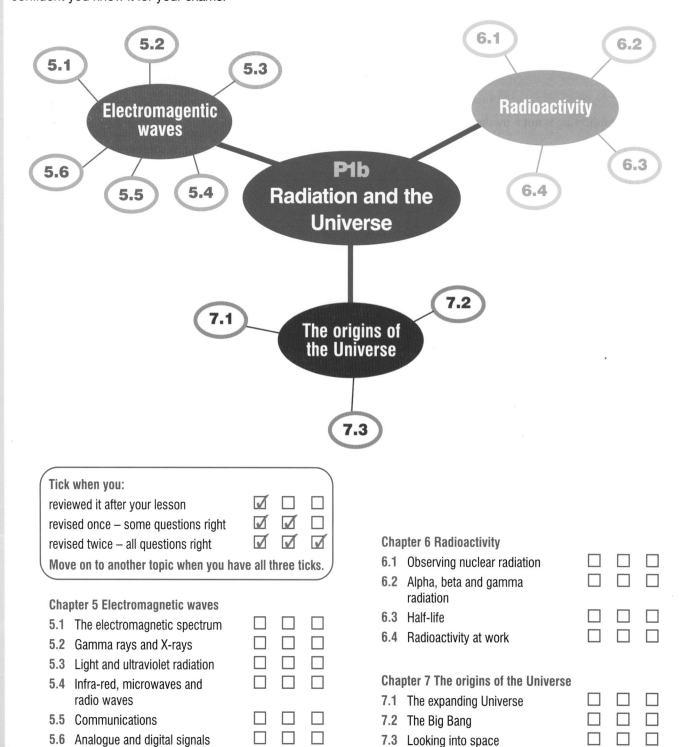

Tick when you:

reviewed it after your lesson	☑	☐	☐
revised once – some questions right	☑	☑	☐
revised twice – all questions right	☑	☑	☑

Move on to another topic when you have all three ticks.

Chapter 5 Electromagnetic waves

5.1	The electromagnetic spectrum	☐	☐	☐
5.2	Gamma rays and X-rays	☐	☐	☐
5.3	Light and ultraviolet radiation	☐	☐	☐
5.4	Infra-red, microwaves and radio waves	☐	☐	☐
5.5	Communications	☐	☐	☐
5.6	Analogue and digital signals	☐	☐	☐

Chapter 6 Radioactivity

6.1	Observing nuclear radiation	☐	☐	☐
6.2	Alpha, beta and gamma radiation	☐	☐	☐
6.3	Half-life	☐	☐	☐
6.4	Radioactivity at work	☐	☐	☐

Chapter 7 The origins of the Universe

7.1	The expanding Universe	☐	☐	☐
7.2	The Big Bang	☐	☐	☐
7.3	Looking into space	☐	☐	☐

What are you expected to know?

Chapter 5 Electromagnetic waves (See students' book pages 282–295)

- Electromagnetic radiation travels as a wave and moves energy from one place to another.

- All electromagnetic waves travel at the same speed through space but have different wavelengths and frequencies.

- The waves together are known as the 'electromagnetic spectrum' and within this they are divided into groups; gamma rays, X-rays, ultraviolet rays, visible light, infra-red rays, microwaves and radio waves.

- When electromagnetic waves move through substances they may be reflected, absorbed or transmitted.

- Different wavelengths of electromagnetic radiation have different effects on living cells.

- There are different uses and hazards for each part of the spectrum.

- Radio waves, microwaves, infra-red and visible light can be used for communication.

- Communication signals can be analogue (continuously varying) or digital (certain values only, usually on or off).

- Electromagnetic waves obey the wave formula:

$$\text{Wave speed} = \text{frequency} \times \text{wavelength}$$

Chapter 6 Radioactivity (See students' book pages 298–307)

- Radioactive substances give out radiation from their nuclei all the time whatever is done to them.

- The three main types of nuclear radiation are alpha particles, beta particles and gamma radiation.

- Properties of alpha particles, beta particles and gamma radiation.

- Half life is the time it takes for the number of parent atoms in a sample to halve.

Chapter 7 The origins of the Universe (See students' book pages 310–317)

- Red shift provides evidence that the Universe is expanding and began with a 'Big Bang'.

- Observations of the Solar System and the galaxies in the Universe can be carried out on the Earth or from space.

- Telescopes used to make observations may detect visible light or other electromagnetic radiations.

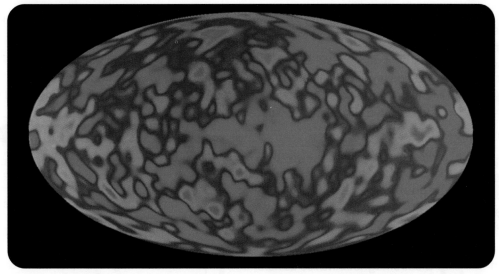

Microwave image of the Universe from COBE, the Cosmic Background Explorer satellite

1. Which part of the electromagnetic spectrum has the longest wavelength?

2. What is the unit of wavelength?

3. How are X-rays used in hospitals?

4. How are gamma rays used in hospitals?

5. How can ultraviolet radiation affect the body?

6. What is visible light?

7. State two uses of microwaves.

8. Which part of the electromagnetic spectrum is detected by night-vision equipment?

9. What is an optical fibre?

10. Which parts of the electromagnetic spectrum are used to carry signals in optical fibres?

11. What is a digital signal?

12. What is meant by 'amplification'?

---

students' book page 282 **P1b 5.1** # The electromagnetic spectrum

KEY POINTS

1 The electromagnetic spectrum (in order of increasing wavelength): gamma rays, X-rays, ultraviolet, visible, infra-red, microwaves, radio waves.

2 All electromagnetic waves travel through space at a speed of 300 million m/s

3 Wave = frequency × wave-
Speed   length
(metres)   (hertz, Hz)   (metres)

Electromagnetic radiations are electric and magnetic disturbances. They travel as waves and move energy from place to place.

All electromagnetic waves travel through space (a vacuum) at the same speed but they have different wavelengths and frequencies.

All of the waves together are called the 'electromagnetic spectrum'. We group the waves according to their wavelength and frequency:

- Gamma rays have the shortest wavelength and highest frequency.
- Radio waves have the longest wavelength and lowest frequency.
- Different wavelengths of electromagnetic radiation are reflected, absorbed or transmitted differently by different substances and types of surface.

Key words: electromagnetic spectrum, wave speed, wavelength, frequency

GET IT RIGHT!

Electromagnetic waves transfer energy, not matter.

EXAM HINTS

Examination questions often come up about the electromagnetic spectrum. Make sure that you can put the parts of the spectrum in the correct order.

CHECK YOURSELF

1 What is the unit of frequency?

2 Which part of the electromagnetic spectrum has the highest frequency?

3 Which part of the electromagnetic spectrum has the shortest wavelength?

Gamma rays and X-rays

GET IT RIGHT!

Gamma radiation can cause cancer but it is also used to treat cancer.

Gamma rays are used to sterilise surgical instruments and keep food fresh for longer by killing the bacteria on it.

X-rays are used to produce shadow pictures of bones (radiographs).

Gamma rays and X-rays mostly pass through soft body tissues, but some is absorbed and will damage the cells. In lower doses, both radiations can cause changes in the cells that make them cancerous. In higher doses, they can kill the cells.

Gamma radiation is used in hospitals, under carefully controlled conditions, to kill cancer cells.

Working with these radiations is hazardous. Gamma sources are kept in thick lead containers. Staff should wear lead aprons and stand behind lead screens when using X-rays. They monitor their exposure to the radiation with film badges.

Key words: Gamma rays, X-rays, dose, cancer

CHECK YOURSELF

1 How does gamma radiation sterilise surgical instruments?

2 Why do workers in X-ray departments wear lead aprons?

3 Why is a radiograph a 'shadow' picture?

Light and ultraviolet radiation

BUMP UP YOUR GRADE

Make sure you can explain in detail some applications and hazards of ultraviolet radiation.

Ultraviolet radiation has a longer wavelength than X-rays. It has a shorter wavelength than the light at the violet end of the visible spectrum.

Ultraviolet radiation from the Sun causes damage to skin cells – tanning, sunburn, skin ageing and skin cancer. Over-exposure can also damage the eyes. Sun beds work by giving out UV rays.

Fluorescent tubes are coated with substances that absorb the ultraviolet radiation produced inside the tube. Then they emit the energy as visible light.

The same substances are used to make hidden security marks that can only be seen with ultraviolet light.

Visible light is the part of the electromagnetic spectrum that is detected by our eyes. We see the different wavelengths within it as different colours. Visible light can be transmitted along optical fibres.

Key words: ultraviolet, fluorescent, visible, optical fibres

CHECK YOURSELF

1 How can the skin be protected from damage by ultraviolet radiation?

2 How do hidden security markings work?

3 Is the frequency of ultraviolet radiation higher or lower than the frequency of X-rays?

Infra-red, microwaves and radio waves

KEY POINTS

1 **Infra-red:** Heaters, communications (remote handsets, optical fibres)
2 **Microwaves:** Microwave oven, communications
3 **Radio waves:** Communications

 EXAMINER SAYS...

Make sure that you can explain the effects of different wavelengths of electromagnetic radiation on living cells.

BUMP UP YOUR GRADE

Knowing the details here is important. It will gain you extra marks and is the difference between a low-grade and a high-grade answer.

- **Infra-red (IR) radiation** is given out by all objects. The hotter the object, the more IR it emits. Night-vision equipment works by detecting this radiation. IR is absorbed by the skin, we sense it as heat and it can burn. It is used as the heat source in toasters, grills and radiant heaters. TV, video and other remote controls use IR. It can be transmitted along optical fibres.
- **Microwaves** are used for cooking and in communications. Microwave ovens produce frequencies that are absorbed by water molecules. They heat the water in food, cooking it from the inside out. The water in living cells will absorb microwaves and they may be damaged or killed by the heat released. Microwave transmitters produce wavelengths that are able to pass through the atmosphere. They are used to send signals to and from satellites and within mobile phone networks.
- **Radio waves** are used to transmit radio and TV programmes. When an alternating voltage is applied to an aerial, it emits radio waves with the same frequency as the alternating voltage. When the waves are received they produce an alternating current with the same frequency as the radiation.

Key words: infra-red radiation, microwaves, radio waves, communications, optical fibres, transmitters

CHECK YOURSELF

1 How can infra-red cameras be used to find survivors after accidents?
2 Why do microwaves cook food from the inside out?
3 How are radio waves produced?

Communications

KEY POINTS

1 The use we make of radio waves depends on the frequency of the waves.
2 Visible light and infra-red radiation are used to carry signals in optical fibres.

GET IT RIGHT!

Remember that the radio wave part of the spectrum covers a large range of frequencies; from 3000 million Hz to less than 300 000 Hz. The range of wavelengths is 0.1 m to more than 1 km.

The microwave and radio wave part of the electromagnetic spectrum is used for communications. This includes terrestrial TV, satellite TV, mobile phones, emergency services radio, amateur radio transmissions, local, national and international radio.

Different frequencies are used for different applications.

Optical fibres are very thin glass fibres. They are flexible and can be bent around curves. Light or infra-red radiation is transmitted along the fibre by continuous reflections.

Key words: communications, optical fibres, reflections

CHECK YOURSELF

1 Which electromagnetic waves are used for transmissions along optical fibres?
2 How are electromagnetic waves transmitted along optical fibres?
3 Which type of electromagnetic wave is used for satellite communications?

P1b 5.6 Analogue and digital signals

KEY POINTS

1 Analogue signals vary continuously in amplitude.
2 Digital signals are either high ('1') or low ('0').
3 Digital transmission, when compared with analogue transmission, is free of noise and distortion. It can also carry much more information.

GET IT RIGHT!

In this context, 'noise' means unwanted, usually random, impulses that get added to the original signal.

Communication signals are either analogue or digital.

- An analogue signal varies continuously in amplitude.
- Digital signals only have certain values. Usually they are either high (on/'1') or low (off/'0'). They can be processed by computers.

When signals are transmitted they become less strong over distance and have to be amplified. They also pick up noise. When amplification takes place the noise is also amplified. With analogue this can make the signal very distorted. With digital the signal can be 'cleaned', because it is still clear which part of the signal is high and which part is low.

Key words: analogue, digital, noise, distortion, amplified

EXAMINER SAYS...

Remember that digital signals can carry much more information than analogue signals. Digital pulses can be made very short so that many pulses can be transmitted each second.

CHECK YOURSELF

1 Why do signals need to be amplified?
2 Why do analogue signals get distorted when they are amplified?
3 Which type of signal can be processed by a computer?

P1b 5   End of chapter questions

1 What are electromagnetic waves?

2 What do all electromagnetic waves have in common?

3 Which part of the electromagnetic spectrum has the lowest frequency?

4 What are gamma rays used for?

5 What is infra-red radiation used for in the home?

6 What is an analogue signal?

7 How are workers in radiography departments in hospitals protected from exposure to X-rays?

8 How does the wavelength of ultraviolet radiation compare with the wavelength of visible light?

9 Why are microwaves dangerous to the body?

10 How does the frequency of radio waves compare with the frequency of visible light?

11 How are optical fibres used in medicine?

12 What is the formula that relates frequency, speed and wavelength?

1. Describe the basic structure of a nucleus.

2. What is the effect of pressure on the rate of radioactive decay?

3. What is the structure of an alpha particle?

4. What is the range of alpha particles in air?

5. What happens to the radioactivity of a sample of a radioactive material over time?

6. What happens to the count rate from a radioactive sample during one half life?

7. Where are alpha sources commonly found in the home?

8. Which is the most dangerous type of nuclear radiation if the source is inside the body?

---

students' book
page 298

P1b 6.1 Observing nuclear radiation

KEY POINTS

1. A radioactive substance contains unstable nuclei.
2. An unstable nucleus becomes stable by emitting radiation.
3. There are three types of radiation from radioactive substances – alpha, beta and gamma radiation.
4. Radioactive decay is a random event – we cannot predict or influence when it will happen.

The basic structure of an atom is a small central nucleus, made up of protons and neutrons, surrounded by electrons.

The atoms of an element always have the same number of protons. However, different isotopes of the element will have different numbers of neutrons.

The nuclei of radioactive substances are unstable. They become stable by radioactive decay. In this process, they emit radiation and turn into other elements.

The three types of radiation emitted are:

- alpha particles
- beta particles
- gamma rays.

Radioactive decay is a random process and is not affected by external conditions.

Key words: nuclei, proton, neutron, radioactive decay, alpha particles, beta particles, gamma rays

GET IT RIGHT!

Radioactive decay is a random process. It is not possible to predict when any particular nucleus will decay and it is not possible to make any particular nucleus decay.

Radioactive decay is not affected by external conditions. So you cannot make it happen faster by changing things like temperature or pressure.

CHECK YOURSELF

1. Which part of an atom might emit alpha particles?

2. What is meant by 'isotopes of an element'?

3. What happens to the rate of radioactive decay if the temperature is doubled?

P1b 6.2 Alpha, beta and gamma radiation

KEY POINTS

1 α-radiation is stopped by paper or a few centimetres of air.
2 β-radiation is stopped by thin metal or about a metre of air.
3 γ-radiation is stopped by thick lead and has an unlimited range in air.

EXAM HINTS

For each of the three types of radiation you need to remember:
- what it is
- how ionising it is
- how far it penetrates different materials
- if it is deflected by electric and magnetic fields.

- **An alpha (α) particle** is a helium nucleus. It is made up of 2 protons and 2 neutrons.
- **A beta (β) particle** is a high-speed electron from the nucleus. It is emitted when a neutron changes to a proton and an electron. The proton remains in the nucleus.
- **Gamma (γ) radiation** is very short wavelength electromagnetic radiation that is emitted from the nucleus.

When nuclear radiation travels through a material it will collide with the atoms of the material and knock electrons off them, creating ions. This is called 'ionisation'.

Alpha particles are relatively large, so they have lots of collisions with atoms – they are strongly ionising. Because of these collisions, the alpha particles do not penetrate far into a material. They can be stopped by a thin sheet of paper, human skin or a few centimetres of air. Alpha particles have a positive charge and are deflected by electric and magnetic fields.

Beta particles are much smaller and faster than alpha particles so they are less ionising and penetrate further. They are blocked by a few metres of air or a thin sheet of aluminium. Beta particles have a negative charge and are deflected by electric and magnetic fields in the opposite sense to alpha particles.

Gamma rays are electromagnetic waves so they will travel a long way through a material before colliding with an atom. They are weakly ionising and very penetrating. Several centimetres of lead or several metres of concrete are needed to absorb most of the radiation. Gamma rays are not deflected by electric and magnetic fields.

Key words: ionisation, electric and magnetic fields, charge

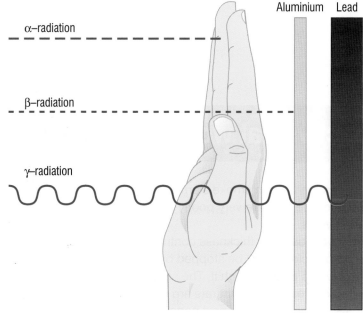

The penetrating powers of α-, β- and γ-radiation

CHECK YOURSELF

1 Which type of nuclear radiation is the most penetrating?

2 Which type of nuclear radiation is the most ionising?

3 Why is gamma radiation not deflected by electric and magnetic fields?

P1b 6.3 Half-life

KEY POINTS

The half-life of a radioactive substance is the time it takes:

1 for the number and (therefore the mass) of parent atoms in a sample to halve
2 for the count rate from the original substance to fall to half its initial level.

BUMP UP YOUR GRADE

Practise doing half-life calculations.

We can measure the radioactivity of a sample of a radioactive material by measuring the count rate from it.

The radioactivity of a sample decreases over time. How quickly the count rate falls to nearly zero depends on the material. Some take a few minutes, others take millions of years.

We use the idea of half-life to measure how quickly the radioactivity decreases. It is the time taken for the count rate from the original substance to fall to half its initial value.

Or we can define it as the time it takes for the number of unstable nuclei in a sample to halve.

The half-life is the same for any sample of a particular material.

Key words: half-life, count rate

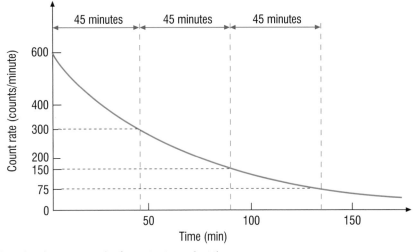

Radioactive decay: a graph of count rate against time

CHECK YOURSELF

1 What happens to the count rate from a sample over time?

2 What has happened to the original count rate of a sample after two half-lives have passed?

3 What has happened to the number of atoms in a sample after two half-lives have passed?

P1b 6.4 Radioactivity at work

KEY POINTS

The use we can make of a radioactive substance depends on:

1 its half life, and
2 the type of radiation it gives out.

- **Alpha sources** are used in smoke alarms. The alpha particles are not dangerous because they are very poorly penetrating. The source needs a half life of several years.
- **Beta sources** are used for thickness control in the manufacture of things like paper. Alpha particles would be stopped by a thin sheet of paper and all gamma rays would pass through it. The source needs a half life of many years, so that decreases in count rate are due to changes in the thickness of the paper. (See diagram on the next page.)

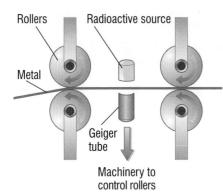

Rollers
Radioactive source
Metal
Geiger tube
Machinery to control rollers

Thickness monitoring using a radioactive source

- **Gamma and beta sources** are used as 'tracers' in medicine. The source is injected or swallowed by the patient. Its progress around the body is monitored by a detector outside the patient. The source needs a half life of a few hours so that the patient is not exposed to unnecessary radioactivity.
- **Gamma sources** are also used to sterilise medical equipment and prevent food spoilage.

If nuclear radiation enters living cells, it causes ionisation which damages cells and may cause cancer.

If the source of radiation is outside the body, alpha particles will be stopped by clothing or skin. Gamma and beta radiation are more dangerous because they may pass through skin and damage cells.

If the source of radiation is inside the body (e.g. it is inhaled), alpha radiation is the most dangerous because it is very strongly ionising.

Key words: tracers

BUMP UP YOUR GRADE

For each radiation you should know an application, why a particular source is used and the approximate half life.

CHECK YOURSELF

1 Why is a beta source less dangerous inside the body than an alpha source?

2 Why do medical tracers have half lives of just a few hours?

3 Why isn't an alpha source used as a tracer in medicine?

P1b 6   End of chapter questions

1 **What is a beta particle?**

2 **What is the range of beta particles in air?**

3 **What is meant by 'half-life'?**

4 **What is gamma radiation?**

5 **Which is the most dangerous type of nuclear radiation if the source is outside the body?**

6 **What happens to the count rate from a radioactive sample during three half-lives?**

7 **Which type of nuclear radiation is the least ionising?**

8 **Which type of nuclear radiation is used for thickness control in the manufacture of paper?**

1. What happens to the sound waves we hear if the source of the waves is moving?

2. Which galaxy is our Sun part of?

3. What happens to light from distant galaxies before it reaches the Earth?

4. How do most scientists think the Universe started?

5. What is a telescope?

6. Where are telescopes used?

KEY POINTS

1. Light from a distant galaxy is red-shifted to longer wavelengths.
2. The further away the galaxy the bigger the red shift.

Galaxies

We live in a galaxy called the Milky Way.

It contains billions of stars

But there are billions of galaxies in the Universe so it is hard to imagine the total number of stars.

GET IT RIGHT!

The further away from us a galaxy is, the faster it is moving away from us.

Red shift

If a source of waves is moving relative to an observer, the wavelength and frequency 'seen' by the observer will have changed (shifted) from the original produced by the source.

This effect can be heard with sound waves. For example the sound of an ambulance siren will sound different depending on whether it is moving towards you (pitch is higher) or away from you (pitch is lower).

The effect occurs with light waves. Light observed from distant galaxies has been 'shifted' towards the red end of the spectrum. This means the frequency has decreased. The further away the galaxy, the bigger the red shift.

This suggests that distant galaxies are moving away from us, and the most distant galaxies are moving the fastest. This is true of galaxies no matter which direction you look in.

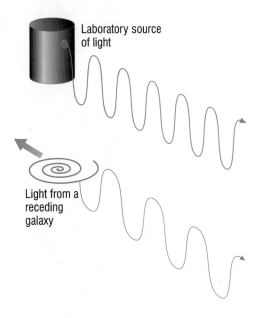

Laboratory source of light

Light from a receding galaxy

Red shift

- Galaxies are collections of billions of stars.
- Our Sun is one of the stars in the Milky Way galaxy.
- The Universe is made up of billions of galaxies.

Key words: red shift, galaxies

CHECK YOURSELF

1 What is a 'galaxy'?

2 What is 'red shift'?

3 Which galaxies are moving away from us fastest?

The Big Bang

KEY POINTS

1 Red shift provides evidence that the Universe is expanding.
2 The Universe started with the Big Bang, a massive explosion from a very small point.

AQA EXAMINER SAYS...

Be sure you can explain why red shift is evidence for an expanding Universe and the Big Bang.

Red shift shows us that distant galaxies are moving away from us and the furthest ones are moving the fastest. This gives us evidence that the Universe is expanding outwards in all directions.

We can try and imagine backwards in time to see where the Universe came from. If it is now expanding outwards, this suggests that it started with a massive explosion at a very small initial point. This is known as the 'Big Bang' theory.

Key words: expanding, Big Bang

The Big Bang

CHECK YOURSELF

1 How does red shift show us that the Universe is expanding?

2 What is meant by the 'Big Bang'?

3 How is an expanding Universe evidence for the Big Bang?

Looking into space

KEY POINTS

1 Observations are made with telescopes that may detect visible light or other electromagnetic radiations.
2 Observations of the Solar System and galaxies can be carried out from the Earth or from space.

GET IT RIGHT!

Not all telescopes detect visible light. Some 'see' into space by detecting radiation from other parts of the electromagnetic spectrum.

Scientists use telescopes to collect the visible light coming from stars, and so see them. They can also use telescopes that collect radiation from other parts of the electromagnetic spectrum such as X-rays, or radio waves. This also allows them to 'see' distant stars.

The atmosphere is a layer of gases surrounding the Earth.

Telescopes on satellites are able to receive all types of electromagnetic radiation from space, without it being distorted or absorbed by the Earth's atmosphere. Because there is no distortion, the pictures produced by these telescopes are clearer and have more detail. So it is possible for us to observe stars that are further away.

A comet

Key words: telescope, atmosphere, satellite

CHECK YOURSELF

1 What is the Earth's atmosphere?

2 What does the Earth's atmosphere do to electromagnetic radiation from space?

3 Why are telescopes on satellites able to produce clearer pictures than those on Earth?

P1b 7 — End of chapter questions

1 **Roughly how many galaxies is the Universe thought to contain?**

2 **What would a 'blue shift' of light from distant galaxies show?**

3 **What evidence is there that the Universe is expanding?**

4 **What has happened to the frequency of light that reaches the Earth from distant galaxies?**

5 **What is the advantage of using a telescope on a satellite rather than on Earth?**

6 **What is a radio telescope?**

1 Which of the following statements about electromagnetic waves is not true?

A They all have the same wavelength.
B They all transfer energy.
C They all travel at the same speed through space.
D They can all travel through a vacuum.

2 The nucleus of an atom contains:

A electrons only
B neutrons only
C protons and neutrons
D protons, neutrons and electrons

3 Which electromagnetic radiation is used in sun beds?

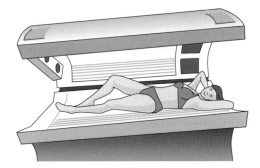

A infra-red
B microwaves
C ultraviolet
D visible light

4 Electromagnetic waves can be grouped according to their frequency.

Match the words A, B, C and D in the list with the spaces (i)–(iv) in the spectrum below:

A infra-red waves   B radio waves
C visible light   D X-rays

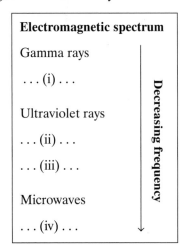

Electromagnetic spectrum	
Gamma rays	
. . . (i) . . .	Decreasing frequency
Ultraviolet rays	
. . . (ii) . . .	
. . . (iii) . . .	
Microwaves	
. . . (iv) . . .	

5 Astronomers study different objects found in the Universe.

Match the words A, B, C and D in the list with the numbers (i)–(iv) in the sentences.

A telescopes   B satellites
C galaxies   D red shift

Astronomers use devices called . . . (i) . . . to allow them to observe different objects. These devices may be positioned on the Earth or on . . . (ii) . . . in space. Astronomers observe distant . . . (iii) . . . and the light from these shows . . . (iv) . . . .

6 The main nuclear radiations are alpha particles, beta particles and gamma rays. They have different properties and uses.

(i) Which nuclear radiation will travel through a thick sheet of paper?
   A alpha particles and beta particles
   B alpha particles only
   C gamma rays and beta particles
   D gamma rays only

(ii) Which nuclear radiation is deflected by electric and magnetic fields?
   A alpha particles and beta particles
   B alpha particles only
   C gamma rays and beta particles
   D gamma rays only

(iii) Which nuclear radiation is the most ionising?
   A alpha particles
   B beta particles
   C gamma rays
   D they are all equally ionising

(iv) Which nuclear radiation is the most penetrating?
   A alpha particles
   B beta particles
   C gamma rays
   D they are all equally penetrating

(v) Which nuclear radiation is the least penetrating?
   A alpha particles
   B beta particles
   C gamma rays
   D they are all equally penetrating

Test & Assessment Interactive quizzes, answers and hints online!

7 For a neutral atom which of the following is always true?

A The number of electrons is greater than the number of neutrons.

B The number of electrons is greater than the number of protons.

C The number of protons is equal to the number of electrons.

D The number of protons is equal to the number of neutrons.

8 The Milky Way is a:

A galaxy

B planet

C solar system

D star

9 Which electromagnetic radiation is used to cook food from the inside out by heating the water molecules in it?

A infra-red

B microwaves

C radio waves

D ultraviolet

10 Radioactive sources are used as tracers in medicine.

Match words A, B, C and D from the list with the numbers (i)–(iv) in the sentences.

A count-rate   B detector

C half-life   D source

The . . . (i) . . . is injected or swallowed by the patient. Its progress around the body is monitored by a . . . (ii) . . . outside the patient which measures the . . . (iii) . . . The source usually has a . . . (iv) . . . of a few hours so that the patient is not exposed to unnecessary radioactivity.

11 An atom contains protons, neutrons and electrons.

Match the words A, B, C and D in the list with the numbers (i)–(iv) in the sentences.

A protons   B neutrons

C electrons   D isotopes

The atoms of an element always have the same number of . . . (i) . . . Different . . . (ii) . . . of the element will have different numbers of . . . (iii) . . . The nucleus is orbited by . . . (iv) . . . .

12 The nuclei of radioactive substances are unstable. They become stable by radioactive decay.

(i) An alpha particle is made up of:

A four neutrons

B four protons

C one proton and one neutron

D two protons and two neutrons

(ii) When the nucleus of a radioactive substance emits an alpha particle it becomes:

A a different element

B a different isotope of the same element

C a lead nucleus

D charged

(iii) A beta particle is:

A an electromagnetic wave

B an electron

C a neutron

D a proton

(iv) Gamma rays are electromagnetic waves from the nucleus of an atom.

They have:

A a long wavelength and a high frequency

B a long wavelength and a low frequency

C a short wavelength and a high frequency

D a short wavelength and a low frequency

Chapter 1

Pre Test

1 Electrical along neurones, chemical across a synapse.   2 In glands.   3 The gap between two neurones.   4 A receptor.   5 28 days (in most women).   6 Follicle stimulating hormone (FSH), oestrogen, luteinising hormone (LH).
7 Luteinising hormone.   8 Follicle stimulating hormone and luteinising hormone.
9 Oestrogen.   10 Follicle stimulating hormone.

Check yourself

1.1
1 Transported by the bloodstream.
2 A gland.   3 Electrical in neurones, chemical across a synapse.
1.2
1 By chemicals.   2 To pass the impulse on to the correct motor neurone.   3 Glands or muscles that make a response.
1.3
1 In the pituitary gland.   2 Oestrogen inhibits the production of FSH and stimulates the production of LH.   3 LH stimulates the release of the mature egg from the ovary.
1.4
1 Oestrogen.   2 FSH stimulates eggs to mature in the ovaries.
1.5
1 We sweat, produce urine and it is in our breath when we breathe out.   2 Our enzymes only work effectively within a narrow temperature range.   3 It is the energy source for respiring cells.

End of chapter questions

1 A stimulus is detected by a receptor.
A sensory neurone is stimulated and carries the impulse to the relay neurone.
The relay neurone passes the impulse to the correct motor neurone.
The motor neurone carries the impulse to an effector (gland or muscle).
The effector makes a response.
Between the neurones the impulse crosses gaps, called synapses, by means of chemicals.
2 The hormone system relies only on messages being transmitted by chemicals. Impulses in the nervous system are electrical, except at synapses where they are chemical. (The hormone system also tends to be slower with the effects being longer lasting.)
3 FSH stimulates both eggs to mature and the release of oestrogen.
Oestrogen inhibits the further production of FSH, stimulates the lining of the womb to build up ready for pregnancy and stimulates the pituitary gland to make LH.
LH stimulates mature eggs to be released.
4 An argument for would be that it allows women (couples) to have children when they would otherwise not be able to. Arguments against might include the cost, it is not 'natural', it is against 'God's will', many eggs may be fertilised but most will 'die', there have been multiple births with most embryos not surviving.
5 Two of: water content, ion content, temperature, blood sugar level.   6 Relay.
7 It contains oestrogen, which inhibits the production of FSH.   8 In the pituitary gland.

Chapter 2

Pre Test

1 Eating the right amounts of the different foods that you need.   2 Not eating the right balance of these different foods (it doesn't just mean not eating *enough* food).   3 The sex they are, how active they are, whether they are pregnant, the temperature they are living in.   4 The rate (speed) that energy is being released from food by the living cells.   5 Obese.   6 Arthritis, diabetes, high blood pressure, heart disease.
7 In the liver.   8 High density and low density (HDLs and LDLs).   9 Saturated fat.   10 High blood pressure.

Check yourself

2.1
1 The rate at which energy is released from food by living cells.   2 Two of: if it is colder, if you are more active, if you are pregnant.
3 You need more energy for the activity. The cells respond by releasing energy from food more quickly.
2.2
1 Obese.   2 A disease of the joints.   3 High blood pressure, diabetes, heart disease.
2.3
1 High blood pressure.   2 They transport cholesterol.   3 Mono-unsaturated and polyunsaturated fats.

End of chapter questions

1 Statins.   2 Saturated fat.   3 Three of: arthritis, diabetes, high blood pressure, heart disease.   4 The rate at which your living cells are releasing energy from food.   5 To replace the heat that you are losing.   6 Reduced resistance to infection or irregular periods for women.   7 Low density lipoprotein.   8 Salt and/or fat.

Chapter 3

Pre Test

1 Against the law.   2 To make very sure that there are no side-effects.   3 As a sleeping pill, but it also helped to prevent 'morning sickness' during pregnancy.   4 The effects of stopping taking a drug on the body.   5 Drugs that people take to stimulate them simply because they want to. They are not being taken for a medical reason.   6 Two of: cannabis, heroin, cocaine.   7 Heroin, cocaine.   8 Nicotine.
9 It is taken up by red blood cells instead of oxygen. You will have less energy or your heart and lungs will have to work harder to compensate.   10 It slows down your reactions.

Check yourself

3.1
1 Leprosy.   2 One of: cannabis, heroin, cocaine, alcohol, tobacco (nicotine).   3 Many more people take them.
3.2
1 Alcohol or tobacco (smoking).   2 Pressure from the people you are with, wanting to experiment further.   3 Many more people take legal drugs.
3.3
1 It slows down your reactions.   2 The brain and liver.   3 Your reactions are slowed so you

take longer to stop. You lose self-control, so you may drive more dangerously or may not be able to judge what is happening on the road very well. You may go into a coma if you have drunk a great deal of alcohol.
3.4
1 There are cancer causing chemicals (carcinogens) in the smoke.   2 Nicotine.
3 They do not get enough oxygen so cannot release as much energy from the food they receive as they should. The carbon monoxide in the smoke reduces the oxygen carrying capacity of the baby's blood.

End of chapter questions

1 It slows it down. Impulses travel more slowly.
2 It reduces the oxygen carrying capacity of the blood. Less energy is released from food. Heart and breathing rate may go up to try to compensate for this.   3 You react more slowly. You may not care as much (lack of self-control). Your judgement will not be as good – both in terms of how you drive and whether you are likely to cause an accident.   4 They are in the tobacco smoke.   5 They need to be tested to see whether they are toxic or have any side effects. Side effects sometimes take many years to be seen.   6 Once a person has tried cannabis he/she may want to try something else, perhaps something more dangerous.
7 Carcinogen.   8 Tobacco or alcohol.

Chapter 4

Pre Test

1 An organism that causes an infectious disease.   2 Bacteria and viruses.   3 Toxins.
4 White blood cell.   5 A chemical that neutralises (cancels out) a toxin (poison).
6 Relieve the symptoms of the disease but they *do not* cure it.   7 A chemical, produced by white blood cells, which helps to destroy pathogens.   8 They live inside the cells. To destroy a virus, you often end up destroying the cell as well.   9 It changes and is resistant to most commonly used antibiotics.
10 A vaccine is made from dead or inactive forms of the pathogen. It is used to give immunity to the person.

Check yourself

4.1
1 Bacteria and viruses.   2 By stopping the transfer of infection from one patient to another.
3 Doctors could not see what was supposed to be causing the infection, they thought it was God's punishment to women, they did not want to admit that they might be responsible for the deaths of patients and hand washing was a strange idea at the time anyway!
4.2
1 By stopping the pathogens entering the body in the first place.   2 They can ingest pathogens and they produce antitoxins, which neutralise the toxins that pathogens produce.   3 They neutralise the toxins.
4.3
1 They kill bacteria but find it more difficult to kill viruses.   2 Viruses live and reproduce inside the body's cells.   3 To alleviate (reduce) the symptoms of the infection (*note:* they do not help to cure the infection).

4.4

1 A disease that spreads across a number of countries. **2** MRSA is resistant to the antibiotics that we normally use. **3** The best-adapted members of a species survive and breed. They pass on their genes. 'Weaker' members of the species do not survive and do not pass on their genes through reproduction.

4.5

1 The drugs have to be tested on volunteers. It can take years for side effects to develop. Until the company is sure there are no side effects, it will not sell the drug. It will cost them a lot of money if it proves to be dangerous. **2** As a sleeping pill and to prevent morning sickness. **3** They believe it is cruel. It causes the animals pain and suffering.

4.6

1 To be injected with a vaccine, which contains dead or inactive forms of the pathogen. **2** The body produces antibodies in response to the vaccine. If the body is infected with the pathogen, it responds very quickly in making antibodies. The disease is destroyed before you even begin to feel ill. **3** If they were not, you might be infected with the disease.

End of chapter questions

1 That infection is spread from one person to another. **2** Pathogens produce toxins (poisons), which make you feel ill. **3** A vaccine contains dead or inactive forms of the pathogen. **4** Antibodies are produced by white blood cells. They help to destroy pathogens in the blood.

5 It means to digest or to destroy them. **6** Penicillin. **7** In the living cells. **8** A change in an organism.

1 (i) D	(ii) A	(iii) C	(iv) B
2 (i) C	(ii) D	(iii) A	(iv) B
3 (i) B	(ii) C	(iii) D	(iv) A
4 (i) A	(ii) B	(iii) D	(iv) C
5 (i) B	(ii) C	(iii) A	(iv) D
6 (i) D	(ii) A	(iii) C	(iv) B
7 (i) D	(ii) A	(iii) B	(iv) B
8 (i) D	(ii) C	(iii) C	(iv) D
9 (i) A	(ii) D	(iii) B	(iv) C

B1b — Answers to questions

Chapter 5

Pre Test

1 Light, water, nutrients. **2** One of: mates, territory. **3** So that it is camouflaged against the snow and ice. It is harder for its prey to see it. **4** The snow and ice has melted. The earth is brown. The prey is camouflaged, so that it is more difficult for its predators to see it. **5** How big the surface area of its skin is compared to the whole size of its body. (This is why a mouse has a large surface area compared to the size of its body, but an elephant has a small surface area compared to the volume of its body.) **6** The heat or the lack of water (and with animals, therefore, the possible lack of food to eat). **7** So that those that eat them know that they have a horrible taste or are poisonous. Once they have tasted them they won't do it again! With animals bright colours are also used to attract a mate. **8** So that they can find enough food (and water). They also need space to breed in. **9** Light, water, nutrients. **10** So that the new plants don't grow alongside them and compete.

Check yourself

5.1

1 It will find it difficult to lose heat, however it will also not heat up as fast as smaller animals. **2** They lose heat through their relatively large surface area quickly and may not be able to find enough food to generate the energy they need. **3** So they are camouflaged against the snow and ice and their prey find it more difficult to see them.

5.2

1 Anywhere where taller plants, e.g. trees, grow. This might be in a forest or woodland. **2** Three of: smaller leaves, water storage in the stem, holes in the leaves (stomata) out of the light and any wind, waxy leaves. **3** The plants may be poisonous or have an awful taste. They have bright colours warning the animals off.

5.3

1 So that they can find enough food (and water). They also need space for breeding. **2** They are showing that they are poisonous or have an awful taste. Once an animal eats it, they will remember the experience! **3** They have long necks, so are able to get to food that other

animals cannot reach. This is particularly important when food is in short supply.

5.4

1 Light, nutrients and water. **2** So that they are able to use the sunlight to grow. Once the trees have their leaves the smaller plants will receive much less light. They will also have much more competition for nutrients and water as the trees begin to grow. **3** If they grow beside the parent plant they will compete with the parent for resources.

End of chapter questions

1 If it eats a plant it doesn't like, and that plant species has a warning colour, it is more likely not to eat that plant again. **2** For mates, food, territory. **3** So that their prey find them more difficult to see. This means that the predator can get closer to its prey before attacking, so there is more chance of success. **4** The heat and the lack of water. **5** To keep them warm in cold seas. **6** One of: very small leaves (spines), stems that photosynthesise, storage of water in the stem. **7** To keep cool / out of the Sun's rays, to catch prey as they cannot be seen to avoid being eaten. **8** They find out which is the slowest, so saving themselves some work.

Chapter 6

Pre Test

1 Male and female sex cells. **2** In the nucleus. **3** Genes (or DNA). **4** Genes from the male and female parent are mixed. **5** It does not lead to any variation. The offspring are genetically identical to the parent. **6** They contain exactly the same genes as the parent. There is no variation (asexual reproduction). **7** You take a group of cells from the plant. You grow them in a special medium, where they develop roots and shoots, before growing them on in soil or compost. **8** Producing identical organisms to the parent through asexual reproduction. **9** Using enzymes. **10** Those against may think it is messing about with nature or that it is in conflict with God's work. Some against feel that the genes that are moved from organism to organism may find their way into other organisms you don't want them to be in, so control is lost. Those in favour feel that it will

result in improved organisms with more of the 'desired' characteristics that we want.

Check yourself

6.1

1 The characteristics of an organism. **2** The information is passed on by the sex cells (gametes) in the genes. **3** In the nucleus.

6.2

1 Sexual reproduction. **2** The genes from both parents are mixed together when the sex cells fuse together. **3** Clones.

6.3

1 Tissue culture and cuttings. **2** The embryo has a certain genetic make up from the parents' sex cells. If you just split the cells apart you are not mixing any new genes into the cells, so they will remain the same as each other and the original embryo. **3** The animal in which the embryo develops.

6.4

1 An adult udder cell. **2** An egg cell. **3** A mild electric shock is applied.

6.5

1 Enzymes are used to cut the gene out. **2** It will develop characteristics associated with the new gene. **3** So that organisms can be developed with the 'desired' characteristics we want, e.g. plants or animals that produce more food or are resistant to disease, etc.

End of chapter questions

1 So that we can produce lots of plants that we want quickly and cheaply and we know that they will be the same as the original plant. **2** The male and female sex cells each have their complement of genes from each parent. When the cells fuse together these genes mix so the offspring is similar to, but not the same as, either parent. **3** Embryo transplants, adult cell cloning, fusion cell. **4** Taking a few cells from a plant and growing them in a special medium so that they develop roots and shoots. The new plant is then grown in the normal way in compost or soil. **5** DNA/genes/chromosomes. **6** There is no mixing of genes / the offspring have the same genetic make-up as the parent. **7** Cuttings, as it is much cheaper and much quicker. **8** Insulin.

Chapter 7

Pre Test

1 All organisms in the same species vary. Some will be more successful and breed. Their genes are passed on to the next generation. Unsuccessful members of the species do not pass their genes on.   2 That if an organism acquired a characteristic, e.g. if a human, through training, developed a fast speed when running, this characteristic would be passed on to the offspring.   3 People can see that we do not pass on these 'acquired characteristics' to the next generation.   4 Many people believed in God and thought that God created new species so the church was very much against Darwin's ideas.   5 They contain the remains of organisms that lived a long time ago. These fossils show that organisms of a species changed only slowly over very long periods of time. In Lamarck's theory, there would be very big changes over very short periods of time.
6 About 3500 million years ago.   7 The ones that are well adapted to their environment and successfully find a mate.   8 Through the sex cells (gametes).   9 When all members of a species 'die out'.   10 A change in a gene.

Check yourself

7.1
1 3500 million years ago.   2 No-one was here and there are two conflicting ideas. Both of these ideas are possible and no-one can either prove one idea or disprove the other one!
3 Through the rocks that they are found in. We can date these rocks.

7.2
1 One which the organism develops while it is alive.   2 Many die out through lack of food, disease, being eaten, being too hot or too cold.
3 They preferred to believe that it was God that created new species.

7.3
1 If new members of the species are produced by sexual reproduction, then the genes from both parents are mixed together when the sex cells fuse.   2 Those that are best adapted or suited to their environment survive and live long enough to breed. The weaker ones do not survive.   3 The organisms best adapted to their environment survive and breed, passing their characteristics on to the next generation.

7.4
1 All of the organisms of the species die out.
2 It may eat all of the food of that species.
3 By hunting them for food, by removing the habitat of the species, through polluting the environment, by introducing new competitors to the species.

End of chapter questions
1 That if an organism acquired a characteristic during its lifetime it could pass this on to its offspring.   2 That simple organisms arrived here from another planet or that conditions on the Earth were such that, along with the energy from lightning, life-forms developed.   3 Two of: competition, disease, new predators, change in the environment, destruction of habitat.   4 We can date rocks. Fossils of previous life-forms are found in rocks.   5 4500 million years.
6 Those that are best adapted to their environment survive and are able to breed.
7 It could fly, swim or be introduced by humans (accidentally or deliberately).   8 Temperature, rainfall.

Chapter 8

Pre Test
1 Once these resources have run out there will be no more as they take so long to be created.
2 Two of: farming, building, quarrying and dumping waste.   3 With sewage, fertiliser, toxic chemicals directly into the water. Pesticides and herbicides can also get washed off the land into water.   4 A substance that enables plants to grow better / replaces nutrients in the soil.   5 Sulfur dioxide.   6 A chemical that kills the pests that can affect plant growth.   7 Invertebrate animals.   8 Carbon dioxide and methane.   9 The trees take in the carbon dioxide for photosynthesis.
10 Development that does not reduce the resources available on the Earth, including land.

Check yourself

8.1
1 Building, quarrying, farming, dumping waste.
2 Pesticides and herbicides.
3 Non-renewable.

8.2
1 Sulfur dioxide and nitrogen oxides.
2 Clouds are blown by the wind so the rain may

fall on another country.   3 Enzymes work best in a very narrow range of acid / alkali conditions (pH). The acidity of the rain stops them working and may denature them.

8.3
1 By cows and by rice fields.   2 Much of the heat of the Sun is radiated back out in to space. Some is absorbed by the atmosphere. The more greenhouse gases there are, the less heat is radiated back into space. The Earth heats up.
3 If trees are cut down, they will not take carbon dioxide up for photosynthesis. If the trees are burned or are left to decompose, then they will release the carbon they contain as carbon dioxide.

8.4
1 The fossil fuels we are using, e.g. petrol, diesel and kerosene, are all non-renewable and will run out.   2 There is only a limited area of land on the Earth. If we keep using more and more, there is less left for other animals and plants.   3 Aluminium is a limited resource. It will eventually run out. It also takes a lot of energy to extract aluminium from its ore.

8.5
1 So as not to destroy too much habitat in the countryside.   2 If they are living in the water you are testing you immediately know it is polluted.   3 Wider.

End of chapter questions
1 Two of: building, farming, quarrying, dumping waste.   2 Lichens.   3 Enzymes.   4 By decomposing (the respiration of the bacteria) or by being burned (combustion).   5 Two of: sewage, fertiliser, toxic chemicals.   6 Carbon dioxide.   7 To kill weeds.   8 Two of: paper, aluminium (cans), plastic, glass.

EXAMINATION-STYLE QUESTIONS

	(i)	(ii)	(iii)	(iv)
1	D	C	A	B
2	A	D	C	B
3	D	A	B	C
4	B	A	D	C
5	C	D	B	A
6	B	D	C	A
7	C	B	D	B
8	D	B	A	D
9	C	C	B	D

C1a   Answers to questions

Chapter 1

Pre Test
1 A compound.   2 Their atoms join with other atoms by giving taking or sharing electrons.
3 As a building material, and to make quicklime, cement and glass. (It has several other uses, but these are the ones you need to know.)
4 Calcium oxide and carbon dioxide.
5 All metal carbonates decompose when heated strongly enough.   6 $MgCO_3 \rightarrow MgO + CO_2$ 7 By adding water to quicklime.
8 Calcium carbonate is formed.   9 By mixing cement, sand, stones or crushed rock and water.   10 To allow light in and to make them weatherproof.

Check yourself

1.1
1 Elements.   2 Atoms (of elements).   3 Two or more elements combined or bonded together.

1.2
1 Building material, to make quicklime, to make cement and to make glass.   2 Breaking down using heat.   3 Three.   4 Five.

1.3
1 Zinc oxide and carbon dioxide.   2 Sodium carbonate and potassium carbonate.
3 $CuCO_3 \rightarrow CuO + CO_2$ 4 10.0 g.

1.4
1 carbon dioxide + calcium hydroxide → calcium carbonate + water   2 $CO_2 + Ca(OH)_2 \rightarrow CaCO_3 + H_2O$ 3 It produces calcium carbonate which is insoluble in water.
4 Calcium hydroxide reacts with carbon dioxide (from the air).

1.5
1 It is stronger, sets faster and sets under water.
2 A mixture of cement, sand, stones or crushed rock and water.   3 By reinforcing with steel.
4 It allows light through (transparent) and is weatherproof (insulator / does not corrode).

End of chapter questions

1 CO_2 and $MgCO_3$. 2 By giving taking or sharing electrons. 3 As a building material, and to make quicklime, cement and glass. 4 calcium carbonate → calcium oxide + carbon dioxide 5 Atoms are not created or destroyed in chemical reactions. 6 Sodium carbonate or potassium carbonate. 7 $Ca(OH)_2 + CO_2 → CaCO_3 + H_2O$ 8 By mixing slaked lime, sand and water. 9 By heating a mixture of limestone and clay. 10 By changing the proportions of the raw materials, and by adding other substances.

Chapter 2

Pre Test

1 Rock that contains enough of a metal or its compounds to make it economic to extract the metal. 2 Displacement, reduction with carbon and electrolysis. 3 Reduction with carbon in a blast furnace. 4 It is iron from the blast furnace that is about 96% iron. 5 It has a regular structure with layers that can slide over each other. 6 Carbon steels, low-alloy steels, high-alloy steels. 7 Metals that contain other elements. 8 Alloys with special properties, such as returning to shape after being bent. 9 Good conductors of heat and electricity, strong, hard and dense, can be bent or hammered into shape, high melting points (except for mercury). 10 By smelting and electrolysis. 11 Low density and resistant to corrosion. 12 High energy costs because of high temperatures and electrolysis.

Check yourself

2.1

1 Rocks that contain enough metal to make it worth extracting. 2 A metal that is found as the metal (not as a compound). 3 Any two metals from zinc, iron, tin, lead, copper (any two in the reactivity series below carbon and above silver). 4 One of: aluminium, magnesium, calcium, sodium or potassium (any metal above carbon in the reactivity series). 5 Oxygen is removed (from a compound).

2.2

1 Iron(III) oxide. 2 Coke. 3 iron oxide + carbon → iron + carbon dioxide
(OR iron oxide + carbon monoxide → iron + carbon dioxide) 4 It is brittle.

2.3

1 Its atoms are in regular layers that can slide over each other. 2 Alloys (mixtures) of iron and other elements. 3 1.5% 4 Low-alloy steel.

2.4

1 Hardness, strength, appearance and resistance to corrosion. 2 Because alloys are mixtures (not compounds). 3 They can return to their original shape (shape memory alloys).

2.5

1 In the central block. 2 They are all metals, good conductors of heat and electricity, strong, hard and dense, can be bent or hammered into shape, have high melting points (except mercury). 3 High-grade ores are running out, existing methods involve moving huge amounts of rock and use large amounts of energy.

2.6

1 Low density and resistance to corrosion. 2 Because it reacts with carbon (which makes it brittle). 3 It is too reactive to extract with carbon. 4 Resources (ores) and energy costs (of extracting the metal) are saved.

End of chapter questions

1 Enough to make it worth extracting. 2 Heat with carbon (displace / heat with a more reactive metal or electrolysis could be used but would be more expensive than using carbon). 3 Oxygen is removed (from iron oxide). 4 It contains (4%) impurities. 5 Iron and carbon. 6 Contains more than 5% of other metals. 7 Changes their properties / makes them more useful. 8 Smart OR shape memory alloys. 9 One of: strong, hard, dense, can be hammered into shape, high melting points. 10 One of: can extract low-grade ores, uses less energy, less rock to be moved / mined (but not just 'cheaper' – too vague). 11 Oxide layer. 12 To extract the (reactive) metal (sodium/magnesium), used to displace titanium.

Chapter 3

Pre Test

1 Hydrogen and carbon.
2 Compounds/(saturated) hydrocarbons with the formula C_nH_{2n+2}. 3 Fractional distillation. 4 Mixtures of compounds with similar boiling points separated from crude oil. 5 Carbon dioxide and water. 6 Carbon monoxide, carbon and unburnt hydrocarbons (particulates), sulfur dioxide. 7 Global warming, global dimming, acid rain. 8 Remove sulfur from fuels, remove sulfur dioxide from waste gases, use alternative fuels.

Check yourself

3.1

1 It is not useful as a fuel / it contains too many substances / substances in it burn under different conditions. 2 Distillation. 3 Compounds of carbon and hydrogen **only**. 4 By molecular formulae and structural formulae.

3.2

1 Fractional distillation. 2 By evaporating the crude oil and condensing the vapours at different temperatures. 3 Hydrocarbons with smallest molecules / lowest boiling points. 4 Those with high boiling points / large molecules / from near the bottom of the column.

3.3

1 Carbon dioxide and water. 2 Carbon monoxide, carbon and unburnt hydrocarbons / particulates. 3 Fuels contain compounds of sulfur.

3.4

1 Carbon dioxide is produced and it is a greenhouse gas. 2 Particles in the atmosphere reflect sunlight away from the Earth. 3 By removing sulfur compounds from fuels at the refinery, or by removing sulfur dioxide from the waste gases after burning.

End of chapter questions

1 It is a mixture (of liquids). 2 C_4H_{10}.
3 Evaporation and condensation. 4 Near the top of the column / tower. 5 propane + oxygen → carbon dioxide + water 6 Carbon and unburnt hydrocarbons. 7 Produces carbon dioxide (which is a greenhouse gas). 8 Sulfur.

EXAMINATION-STYLE QUESTIONS

	(i)	(ii)	(iii)	(iv)
1	B	D	C	A
2	D	B	A	C
3	B	D	A	C
4	C	B	A	D
5	C	D	A	B
6	C	D	B	A
7	B	D	B	A
8	B	D	D	B
9	B	B	B	D

C1b   Answers to questions

Chapter 4

Pre Test

1 Breaking down by heat (thermal decomposition) of large hydrocarbon molecules to make smaller molecules. 2 (Unsaturated) hydrocarbons with a carbon–carbon double bond ($C=C$). 3 A substance with long chain (very large) molecules made by joining many small molecules (monomers). 4 By addition polymerisation using ethene as the monomer. 5 Softens whenever it is heated. 6 It sets hard (chemical bonds form between the polymer chains). 7 By changing the monomers, by changing the reaction conditions when they are made. 8 Two of: food packaging / drinks bottles / breathable waterproof fabrics / medical uses / hydrogels / shape memory polymers / smart polymers.

Check yourself

4.1

1 (Catalytic) thermal decomposition. 2 Hot catalyst. 3 Unsaturated hydrocarbons / hydrocarbons with a double bond / general formula C_nH_{2n}. 4 Use bromine water – turns colourless.

4.2

1 Small molecules that join together to make polymers. 2 Poly(ethene). 3 The monomers add together to form the polymer and no other product is formed. 4 As plastics, e.g. bags, bottles, containers, toys.

4.3

1 They have very long molecules that tangle together. 2 It softens when it is heated (every time). 3 Chemical (strong) bonds are formed between the polymer chains.
4 Thermosoftening.

4.4

1 By changing the monomers / by changing the reaction conditions. 2 They keep food in good condition (or a specific property such as waterproof / transparent / do not tear easily / lightweight). 3 They can make fabrics that are waterproof but that are also able to let gases

through (breathable).   4 One from: hydrogel, smart polymer, shape memory polymer.

End of chapter questions

1 To make smaller, more useful molecules / to make alkenes / to make smaller alkanes (for use as fuels).   2 They have two fewer hydrogen atoms / they have a double bond / they are more reactive / they react with bromine water.   3 Many monomers add / join together to form the polymer with no other product.   4 Propene / butene / pentene / hexene, etc.   5 Weak intermolecular forces.   6 The strong chemical bonds cannot be easily broken so it does not soften when heated.   7 Two of: lighter weight / flexible or not brittle or do not break easily.   8 Hydrogels.

Chapter 5

Pre Test

1 Foods and fuels.   2 By pressing or by distillation.   3 It cooks faster in oil than in water, because the oil is at a higher temperature than boiling water.   4 It has been reacted with hydrogen to remove the carbon–carbon double bonds ($C=C$) and make it saturated so that it is solid at room temperature.   5 A mixture of tiny droplets of immiscible liquids suspended in each other.   6 To prevent the liquids in the emulsion from separating.   7 A substance added to food to preserve it or to improve colour, flavour or texture.   8 These show additives permitted in the European Union.   9 Vegetable oil that can be used as fuel for diesel engines.   10 Renewable and cleaner / less harmful to the environment (less pollution).

Check yourself

5.1

1 Pressing and distillation (with water added).   2 They produce a lot of energy.   3 An oil with molecules that contain carbon–carbon double bonds (so they contain fewer hydrogen atoms than the corresponding saturated molecule).   4 Bromine water.

5.2

1 The temperature of hot oil is higher than boiling water.   2 Taste, colour, texture and energy content.   3 Addition reaction.   4 To make them solid at room temperature.

5.3

1 By vigorously mixing (stirring, shaking or beating) two liquids that do not usually mix

together.   2 They keep the droplets suspended because different parts of their molecules are attracted to each of the liquids.   3 Thicker and more opaque / not transparent.

5.4

1 To preserve it, to improve colour, flavour and texture.   2 To show they are permitted additives (in the EU).   3 They would be listed in the ingredients.   4 They can be chemically analysed (using chromatography, mass spectrometry etc.).

5.5

1 It is produced from plants / crops that can be planted again.   2 Waste vegetable oil can be modified to use as diesel fuel (instead of dumping it or just burning it).   3 It produces less pollution (no additional carbon dioxide, no sulfur dioxide), more biodegradable than fossil fuels.

End of chapter questions

1 The plant material is pressed and water and impurities are removed.   2 Use bromine water (it turns from orange-yellow to colourless).   3 Some of the oil is absorbed by the food.   4 Hydrogenation (reaction / addition of hydrogen using a catalyst).   5 Liquids that do not mix / dissolve in each other / are immiscible.   6 Salad dressings (mayonnaise) ice cream, milk, sauce.   7 Preservatives.   8 Chromatography.   9 The carbon dioxide released on burning was removed by plants as they grew.   10 Biodiesel is biodegradable / breaks down faster / less toxic.

Chapter 6

Pre Test

1 Crust, mantle and core.   2 Between 5 km and 70 km thick.   3 The crust and upper part of the mantle (the lithosphere).   4 At the bottom of the oceans (mid-oceanic ridges).   5 Carbon dioxide.   6 By (green) plants.   7 Nitrogen.   8 Noble gases.   9 Respiration, decomposition and combustion.   10 Photosynthesis, dissolving.

Check yourself

6.1

1 0.005 to 0.07 cm (or 0.05 to 0.7 mm).   2 Outer core is liquid, inner core is solid.   3 They thought the crust solidified and then the Earth cooled further causing it to shrink and the crust to wrinkle.

6.2

1 Large pieces of the Earth's crust and upper mantle (lithosphere).   2 Radioactivity releases heat that causes convection currents in the mantle, which move the plates.   3 Mountains form, earthquakes and volcanoes.   4 He could not explain why continents move / he was not a geologist.

6.3

1 Volcanoes.   2 It condensed to form the oceans.   3 Photosynthesis.

6.4

1 About 200 million years.   2 Argon.   3 In sedimentary rocks and fossil fuels.   4 They are very unreactive.

6.5

1 It returns to the atmosphere when animals respire or plants and animals die and decompose.   2 Dissolving in the oceans.   3 Burning fossil fuels.

End of chapter questions

1 0.5%   2 It is under the crust, about 3000 km thick / goes almost halfway to the centre, almost entirely solid, but can flow very slowly.   3 As plates move, huge forces are produced that cause the crust to crumple / buckle / deform.   4 New evidence from observations on the ocean floor.   5 Three from: Carbon dioxide, nitrogen, water vapour, methane, ammonia.   6 Plants absorbed carbon dioxide to make food. Animals ate plants and produced shells that formed sedimentary rocks. Some plant and animal remains produced fossil fuels.   7 Noble gases (helium, neon, argon, krypton, xenon), carbon dioxide and water vapour.   8 It is less dense than air and it is not flammable / does not burn.   9 By heating up carbonate rocks (that have moved underground).   10 Carbon dioxide dissolves in the water.

EXAMINATION-STYLE QUESTIONS

	(i)	(ii)	(iii)	(iv)
1	D	C	A	B
2	B	C	D	A
3	B	A	D	C
4	D	B	C	A
5	C	D	B	A
6	C	D	B	C
7	C	C	B	C
8	D	D	A	D
9	B	C	A	B

P1a   Answers to questions

Chapter 1

Pre Test

1 Radiation.   2 Radiation.   3 White surfaces are poor absorbers of thermal radiation, so a house that has been painted white will stay cooler.   4 A light, shiny teapot will keep tea hot the longest.   5 In metals the normal conduction process occurs, but heat energy is also passed through the metal by free electrons.   6 An insulator is a poor conductor – it does not allow heat energy to pass through it easily.   7 Convection.   8 Convection is the movement of heat energy through a fluid (liquid or gas) by

convection currents, caused by changes in its density due to temperature differences.   9 Convection.   10 Conduction.

Check yourself

1.1

1 Infra-red.   2 By radiation through space.   3 No, the hotter an object the more heat it radiates.

1.2

1 The best emitters of heat radiation are dark, matt surfaces.   2 The best absorbers of heat radiation are dark, matt surfaces.   3 To maximise the amount of heat they radiate.

1.3

1 Air is a poor conductor, so materials that trap air are good insulators.   2 Metal is a good conductor so the food is heated quickly, the wooden handle is a good insulator so you will not get burnt when you pick the saucepan up.   3 The best conductors of heat are metals.

1.4

1 Convection occurs in fluids.   2 The density decreases.   3 The particles in a solid are not free to move.

1.5

1 Conduction. **2** It traps air in small pockets, so it reduces convection. **3** Loft insulation is usually made from fibreglass.

End of chapter questions

1 Conduction, convection and radiation.
2 Conduction. **3** The bottom of the fluid is heated, it becomes less dense and rises and is replaced by colder, denser fluid which in turn is heated and rises. **4** If one end of the metal is heated the particles at that end gain kinetic energy and vibrate more. This energy is passed to neighbouring particles and in this way the heat is transferred through the metal. Also the free electrons in the metal gain kinetic energy and move through the metal, transferring energy by colliding with other particles. **5** Its surface area, the type of surface and its temperature compared to the surroundings. **6** Conduction involves particles vibrating and passing their energy to neighbouring particles, in a gas the particles are not held closely together. **7** It has no effect. **8** A large surface area increases the amount of radiation. **9** Concrete conducts heat away from your feet, so they feel cold. The carpet is an insulator. **10** The jacket is an insulator and reduces heat losses from the tank keeping the hot water hotter for longer.

Chapter 2

Pre Test

1 Gravitational potential energy. **2** Movement energy. **3** Sound energy to electrical energy. **4** Energy cannot be created or destroyed, only changed from one form to another. **5** Electrical energy to kinetic energy. **6** It is transferred to the surroundings, which become warmer. **7** Efficiency does not have a unit. **8** The joule, J.

Check yourself

2.1
1 Elastic potential (strain) energy. **2** From the food you eat. **3** Kinetic energy.
2.2
1 Chemical energy into heat energy.
2 Electrical energy to light and heat energy.
3 Chemical energy in the muscles, from the food you eat, is turned into kinetic energy.
2.3
1 The useful energy transformation is from electrical energy to light, energy is wasted as heat which warms the surroundings.
2 It becomes difficult to collect the spreading heat energy to turn it into other forms of energy.
3 Devices have vents so that wasted energy in the form of heat warms the surroundings. Otherwise the device would overheat.
2.4
1 The efficiency goes up.

2 Efficiency $= \dfrac{5\,J}{20\,J} = 0.25$ (25%)

3 Efficiency $= \dfrac{(5000 - 2000)}{5000} = 0.6$ (60%)

End of chapter questions

1 Gravitational potential energy – book on a shelf.
  Elastic potential energy – in a stretched bungee rope.
  Chemical energy – stored in a piece of coal.
2 Chemical energy in your muscles is changed to kinetic energy as you move, and this is changed into gravitational potential energy as you climb higher above the ground. When you

fall, gravitational potential energy is changed into kinetic energy and this is changed to heat and some sound as you hit the ground. **3** In an electric heater, the useful energy change is to heat energy. As this is the same as the wasted energy, the device can be 100% efficient.

4 Efficiency $= \dfrac{720\,000\,J}{750\,000\,J} = 0.96$ (96%)

5 The energy not used to heat the water heats the body of the kettle and the surroundings.
6 Elastic potential energy. **7** Electrical energy to kinetic energy. **8** Light to electrical energy.

Chapter 3

Pre Test

1 Electrical energy to heat energy.
2 Electrical energy to light and heat energy.
3 The power of a device is the rate at which it transforms energy. **4** watt, W. **5** kilowatt-hour. **6** Energy transferred = power of device × time in use **7** The National Grid is a network of transformers, pylons and cables that connects power stations to homes, schools offices and other buildings. **8** A step-up transformer.

Check yourself

3.1
1 Electrical energy to kinetic energy. **2** From chemical energy that is stored in a battery then changed to electrical energy. **3** Electrical energy to kinetic energy and thermal energy.
3.2
1 30 000 **2** 2.5 kW = 2500 W. So the 3000 W heater is more powerful.

3 Power $= \dfrac{36\,000\,J}{3 \times 60\,s} = 200\,W$

3.3
1 Power
2 Energy transferred = 9 kW × 20/60 h = 3 kWh
3 Energy transferred = 0.1 kW × 4 h = 0.4 kWh
  Cost = 8 p × 0.4 kWh
  Cost = 3.2 p
3.4
1 A Step-down transformer. **2** High voltages reduce energy losses in the cables of the National Grid, making the system more efficient. **3** A Step-down transformer.

End of chapter questions

1 Joule per second, J/s **2** Microphone.
3 Speaker. **4** 3000 J.

5 Power $= \dfrac{36\,000\,000\,J}{1 \times 60 \times 60\,s}$
$= 10\,000\,W = 10\,kW$

6 Energy transferred = 1.2 kW × 10/60 h
= 0.2 kWh
  Cost = 0.2 kWh × 7p per kWh = 1.4 p
7 See diagram on page 85. **8** The higher voltages used in the Grid would be dangerous in the home.

Chapter 4

Pre Test

1 Coal, oil and gas. **2** Uranium/plutonium.
3 Falling water. **4** An electricity generator on top of a tall tower with blades that rotate when the wind passes over them. **5** A solar cell produces electricity from light. **6** Geothermal energy is energy released by radioactive substances deep inside the Earth, which heats

the surrounding rocks. **7** Wind energy, wave energy. **8** A nuclear power station does not produce greenhouse gases.

Check yourself

4.1
1 Plutonium. **2** Nuclear fission. **3** The steam drives turbines that rotate generators and produce electricity.
4.2
1 The energy source for a hydroelectric power station is falling water, so the station must be built at the bottom of a hill for the water to fall. **2** Gravitational potential energy. **3** The tides always go in and out twice a day. Waves are generated by the wind so if there is no wind there are few waves.
4.3
1 Geothermal energy comes from radioactive processes in the rocks deep in the Earth.
2 Light energy to electrical energy. **3** A single solar cell only produces a small amount of electrical energy, even when the Sun is shining brightly, so to power larger devices many cells are joined.
4.4
1 Non-renewable. **2** Gas and hydro-electric power stations. **3** A large, flat, exposed area away from housing.

End of chapter questions

1 Renewable energy resources can be produced at the same rate as they are used up. Non-renewable energy resources are used up at a much faster rate than they can be produced.
2 Energy from falling water, waves and tides.
3 In a few parts of the world, hot water produced by geothermal energy comes up to the surface naturally and can be piped to nearby buildings to heat them.
  In other places, very deep holes are drilled down to the hot rocks. Cold water is pumped down to the hot rocks where it is heated and comes back to the surface as steam. It is used to drive turbines and produce electricity.
4 Fossil fuels are a reliable energy resource. Gas-fired power stations can be started up quickly in order to cope with periods of sudden demand. **5** Fossil fuels are non-renewable so they will run out in the near future. Fossil fuels produce polluting gases such as CO_2 and SO_2.
6 Produces nuclear waste that is difficult to dispose of and there is a risk of a major accident if nuclear radiation escapes. **7** Using geothermal energy in most places requires drilling large distances through cooler rock to reach the hot rocks. Unless the hot rocks are relatively close to the surface this is too expensive. **8** Black, for better absorption of radiation.

EXAMINATION-STYLE QUESTIONS

1	B			
2	C			
3	A			
4	(i) D	(ii) B	(iii) A	(iv) C
5	(i) A	(ii) C	(iii) B	(iv) D
6	(i) D	(ii) B	(iii) A	(iv) C
7	D			
8	C			
9	C			
10	D			
11	(i) C	(ii) D	(iii) B	(iv) A
12	(i) A	(ii) B	(iii) C	(iv) D
13	(i) D	(ii) A	(iii) A	(iv) B

Chapter 5

Pre Test
1 Radio waves.   2 Metre, m.   3 X-rays are used to take shadow pictures of bones.
4 Gamma rays are used to kill cancer cells.
5 Ultraviolet radiation can tan the skin. It can also cause sunburn, skin ageing, skin cancer and damage to the eyes.   6 Visible light is the part of the electromagnetic spectrum that is detected by the eyes.   7 For cooking and communications.   8 Infra-red radiation.
9 A very thin glass fibre.   10 Visible light and infra-red radiation.   11 Sequence of pulses that are (usually) either on (1) or off (0).
12 The strengthening of a signal.

Check yourself
5.1
1 Hertz, Hz.   2 Gamma rays.   3 Gamma rays.
5.2
1 Gamma rays kill bacteria.   2 The lead absorbs X-rays.   3 Bones absorb X-rays but they pass through soft tissue. So the areas on an X-ray film that are *not* exposed show where the bones are.
5.3
1 By covering with clothing or suncream.
2 The markings are invisible when viewed under visible light, but show up when an ultraviolet light is shone on them.   3 Lower.
5.4
1 Infra-red cameras detect infra-red radiation given out by the survivors' bodies which are warmer than the surroundings.   2 Microwaves are strongly absorbed by the water molecules inside food, heating them.   3 Radio waves are produced by applying an alternating voltage to an aerial.
5.5
1 Visible light and infra-red radiation.
2 By continuous reflections along the fibre.
3 Microwaves.
5.6
1 Signals weaken over distance.   2 Noise picked up by the signal is amplified along with the original signal.   3 Digital

End of chapter questions
1 Electromagnetic waves are electric and magnetic disturbances that travel as waves and move energy from place to place.   2 They all travel at the same speed in a vacuum.
3 Radio waves.   4 Sterilising surgical instruments, keeping food fresh by killing bacteria on it and killing cancer cells.   5 TV and video remote controls and cooking food.
6 A signal that varies continuously in amplitude.
7 They wear lead aprons and stand behind lead screens when taking X-rays.   8 The

wavelength is shorter.   9 Microwaves are strongly absorbed by the water in the cells, causing heating and damage.   10 The frequency is lower.   11 Optical fibres are passed into the body and light is transmitted along them so that images of the inside of the body can be seen.   12 Speed = frequency × wavelength

Chapter 6

Pre Test
1 A small central nucleus made up of protons and neutrons, surrounded by electrons.   2 It has no effect.   3 An alpha particle consists of 2 protons and 2 neutrons.   4 A few centimetres.   5 It decreases.   6 It decreases to half the original value.   7 In smoke alarms.
8 Alpha particles.

Check yourself
6.1
1 The nucleus.   2 Isotopes of an element have the same number of protons, but different numbers of neutrons, in the nucleus.
3 Nothing, the rate of decay is independent of the temperature.
6.2
1 Gamma rays.   2 Alpha particles.
3 Gamma radiation is an electromagnetic wave from the nucleus.
6.3
1 It decreases.   2 It has decreased to one quarter of its original value.   3 It has decreased to one quarter of its original value.
6.4
1 It is less ionising than alpha radiation.
2 The half life must be long enough to complete the medical procedure, but short enough to avoid exposing the patient for longer than is necessary.   3 Alpha particles are very poorly penetrating so they would not be detected outside the body.

End of chapter questions
1 A beta particle is an electron from the nucleus.   2 A few metres.   3 The time it takes for the number of radioactive atoms in a sample to halve.   4 Gamma radiation is a high frequency electromagnetic wave emitted from the nucleus of an atom.   5 Gamma rays.   6 It drops to 1/8 of the original value.   7 Gamma rays.   8 Beta particles.

Chapter 7

Pre Test
1 The sound waves you hear would be a different frequency (pitch) to the sound waves emitted by the source.   2 The Milky Way.

3 Its frequency changes.   4 With a massive explosion at a very small initial point – the Big Bang.   5 A device that collects light or other electromagnetic radiations so distant objects can be observed.   6 Telescopes are used on the Earth or on satellites in space.

Check yourself
7.1
1 A galaxy is a collection of millions of stars.
2 Red shift is the changing of the frequency of light from distant galaxies towards the red end of the spectrum, because they are moving away from us.   3 The most distant ones.
7.2
1 It shows us that distant galaxies are moving away from us, and the furthest ones are moving the fastest, so the Universe is expanding outwards in all directions.   2 The massive explosion that was the start of the Universe.
3 If the Universe is now expanding outwards in all directions, this suggests that it started with an explosion from a single point.
7.3
1 The layer of gas that surrounds the Earth.
2 It absorbs and scatters it.   3 The signals received by telescopes on satellites are not distorted by the atmosphere.

End of chapter questions
1 Billions.   2 A blue shift would show that they are moving towards us.   3 Distant galaxies are moving away from us, the most distant galaxies are moving the fastest and this is true of galaxies no matter which direction you look.   4 The frequency has decreased.
5 The images produced are clearer.
6 A telescope that collects radio waves rather than visible light.

EXAMINATION-STYLE QUESTIONS

1	A				
2	C				
3	C				
4	(i) D	(ii) C	(iii) A	(iv) B	
5	(i) A	(ii) B	(iii) C	(iv) D	
6	(i) C	(ii) A	(iii) A	(iv) C	(v) A
7	C				
8	A				
9	B				
10	(i) D	(ii) B	(iii) A	(iv) C	
11	(i) A	(ii) D	(iii) B	(iv) C	
12	(i) D	(ii) A	(iii) B	(iv) C	